ABSOLUTE KNOWLEDGE THAT LIBERATES CONSCIOUSNESS

AN EXPLANATION OF HIGHER REALITIES

What to Know About Your Essence of Being, Relationship With the Infinite, and Ultimate Spiritual Destiny

Roy Eugene Davis

CSA Press   Lakemont, Georgia

ISBN 0-87707-297-3

CSA Press
Post Office Box 7
Lakemont, Georgia 30552-0001

Tel: 706-782-4723
Fax: 706-782-4560
e-mail: csainc@csa-davis.org
Web Site: www.csa-davis.org

CSA Press is the publishing department
of Center for Spiritual Awareness

Printed in the United States of America

I salute the supreme teacher, the Truth,
whose nature is bliss; the giver of the
highest happiness; pure wisdom;
beyond all qualities and infinite like
the sky; beyond words; one and eternal;
pure and still; beyond all change and
phenomena; and the silent witness
to our thoughts and emotions.
I salute Truth, the supreme teacher.
— *Ancient Vedic Hymn*

PARAMAHANSA YOGANANDA

ABSOLUTE KNOWLEDGE THAT LIBERATES CONSCIOUSNESS

The Author's Books Published by CSA Press

Paramahansa Yogananda As I Knew Him
Seven Lessons in Conscious Living (Kriya Yoga Practices)
The Science of Self-Realization (Patanjali's yoga-sutras)
A Master Guide to Meditation & Spiritual Growth
Satisfying Our Innate Desire to Know God
The Science of God-Realization
An Easy Guide to Ayurveda
The Eternal Way (The Inner Meaning of the Bhagavad Gita)

United Kingdom (Distributor)
Gazelle Book Services LTD sales@gazellebooks.co.uk

India
Motilal Banarsidass, Delhi. mlvd@vsnl.com www.mlbd.com
Full Circle, New Delhi. www.atfullcircle.com
B. Jain Books, New Delhi. www.bjainbooks.com

Germany
Pfad des Lichts
Paramahansa Yogananda – wie ich ihn kannte
www.kriya-yoga.de

Italy
Paramahansa Yogananda Così come l'ho conosciuto
La scienza della realizzazione del sé
La strada maestra per la meditazione e la crescita spirituale
Marco Valerio Editore. www.marcovalerio.com

Preface

An Invitation to Discovery

The acquired habit of identifying with ordinary states of mind and consciousness and objective circumstances causes people to have mistaken ideas about themselves and their relationship with the Infinite. Not knowing the truth about their essence of being, and the Reality commonly referred to as God, they are inclined to think irrationally and allow behaviors to be determined by flawed beliefs, subconscious inclinations, habits, trends of random events, or the opinions or actions of others.

I was fortunate during my late teenage years to discover the philosophical principles described in the following pages, be personally taught by my guru, Paramahansa Yogananda, and be inspired and highly self-motivated to live with a clear sense of meaningful purpose.

Because of the insights and experiences I have had during the past several decades, I can attest to the authenticity and practical usefulness of this information. It is my hope that your own comprehension of these facts of life will be psychologically and spiritually transformative.

ROY EUGENE DAVIS

May 2007
Lakemont, Georgia

Word Meanings to Know

absolute Perfect in nature or quality: complete. Not mixed: pure. Unlimited by restrictions or exceptions: unconditional.

knowledge Comprehension acquired by study or experience.

liberates Releases from conditions that confine or limit.

consciousness The capacity to be self-aware, observe, and perceive. The totality of one's memories, thoughts, beliefs, and sensitivities to respond or react to objective or subjective conditions.

The Text

Some of the chapters are revised versions of articles that were earlier published in the author's *Studies in Truth* lessons for his students and in the Center for Spiritual Awareness *Truth Journal* magazine.

Glossary

Refer to it as often as may be necessary to understand the meanings of words and philosophical concepts used in the text.

Calendar Eras Mentioned In the Text

BCE (before the current era) and CE (current era) are used instead of B.C. and A.D.

Contents

ABSOLUTE KNOWLEDGE THAT LIBERATES CONSCIOUSNESS

Chapter 1

The Truth About Your Essence of Being and Your Relationship With the Infinite

To know the truth about your essence of being and your relationship with the Infinite, all erroneous concepts and opinions that interfere with rational thinking and endeavors to intellectually and intuitively comprehend the facts of life will have to be discarded.

Unwavering resolve to have accurate knowledge of higher realities, and practical application of the lifestyle regimens and spiritual practices recommended in this book, will free you from all conditions that confine your awareness and interfere with your endeavors to be creatively expressive.

Every person is impelled by an innate urge—that arises from the depths of their essence of being—to consciously, joyously live forever without limitations. When this desire is so compelling that its fulfillment becomes the primary aim, one is then ready to be fully dedicated to an intentional course of action that will allow their innate qualities and capacities to quickly be fully actualized.

Ordinary human existence determined by provincial ways of thinking and behaving is not fully satisfying and is never spiritually beneficial. Most people are born, aimlessly live for a few decades, and die without having seriously thought about their spiritual well-being or having done anything to be more conscious and freely functional. They experience their brief incarnation as though dreaming and allow circumstances to be determined by their erratic behaviors or random events.

13

The One Reality Commonly Referred to As God

The absolute essence of the one Reality is pure existence beyond space and time, devoid of characteristics. Most of the names that have been used to define or describe it are the concepts of people whose knowledge of it is flawed or who personalize it to satisfy their emotional needs. People who are emotionally mature and intellectually curious tend to welcome information that is supported by valid knowledge about the one Reality.

The expressive modes of the one Reality are the attributes which produce universes and regulate their orderly processes. The word *god*, is from Old German "the highest good." Lord, Heavenly Father, The Almighty, and other names are used to indicate imagined or perhaps partially discerned attributes of the supreme Reality. Divine Mother, a name sometimes used by people whose psychological temperament is devotional, is used in India and other regions of the world to indicate nature's creative, transformative influences.

That which is permanently real can be partially, intellectually known; more clearly known when intuitively perceived; and fully known by having direct experience of it.

Your Relationship With God

As a pure-conscious unit of a larger Reality, you are an immortal spiritual being with innate potential to bring forth and use exceptional powers of perception and extraordinary functional abilities. With patient resolve to learn, you can know the truth about the facts of life and be empowered to live freely. Your exemplary life will then inspire others, and the silent radiance of your illumined consciousness will elevate the consciousness of everyone.

To merely acquire information about the facts of life is not redemptive. What is needed is accurate perception of what is observed, and the unveiling of innate knowledge that will spontaneously emerge as a revelation from the innermost level of your essence of being.

All knowledge of the one Reality is within it. Because you are an individualized unit of that Reality, knowledge of it and its processes is within you. As your innate knowledge is progressively, or perhaps quickly, unveiled, all of your spiritual qualities and capacities will become fully actualized. You will then clearly see what you did not formerly see, know what you did not formerly know, and be constantly inspired and empowered to do what you could not formerly do.

Why You Are In This World

You came into this world from deep, inner space and to it you will eventually return. You did not come here to merely complacently exist for a few decades, satisfy mundane desires and needs, enjoy a few personal relationships while they last, struggle to survive, cope with problems and random events, and depart without being conscious of your real nature and relationship with the Infinite. You are here to skillfully relate to the physical environment, improve your intellectual and functional capacities, live effectively with a well-defined sense of purpose, and quickly awaken through the remaining stages of your spiritual growth.

The four primary aims to have actualized are:

- *To live in harmony with natural laws with a clear sense of meaningful purpose.* You can do this by effectively using your knowledge and skills while allowing the inclination of supreme Consciousness to support and provide for you. All of your thoughts and actions will also be fully supportive of others who are influenced by what you do.
- *To have your life-enhancing desires easily fulfilled.* Desires

can be satisfied by performance of productive actions and by using imagination and intention to produce and attract ideal events and circumstances. Your mind is a unit of cosmic mind which is responsive to your mental states, thoughts, feelings, and intentions. Firmly believe that you can do what you want to do, experience what you want to experience, and have what you need or want to have. Do what can be done to satisfy life-enhancing desires. Cosmic mind and impulses of grace will do what you cannot do.

By attentive experimentation, acquire knowledge of the physical, mental, and spiritual laws of cause and effect: the procedural principles applicable in their domains or fields.

Physical actions produce physical effects.

Thoughts, desires, imagination, beliefs, and intentions can cause effects and attract events and circumstances.

Your awareness of your relationship with the Infinite attracts fortunate events and circumstances.

- *To have a continuous flow of material resources to satisfy your needs and enable you to accomplish purposes that are of value.* Avoid thinking that there is a difference between spiritual and material realities. Be receptive to the good fortune that can be yours.
- *To be fully Self-realized and liberated.* To realize something is to have direct experience and accurate knowledge of it. You will be Self-realized when you experience and know your true nature as it is. You will be God-realized when you experience and know God as God is. When your consciousness is purified, you will be liberated.

The two stages of liberation are: 1) being Self-realized while subconscious conditions are still somewhat influential or have the potential to be influential; 2) Self-realization which is not influenced by subconscious conditions or external circumstances, along with flawless knowledge of higher realities.

How Absolute Knowledge Liberates Consciousness

Partial knowledge of your true nature and higher realities may be mixed with false ideas and illusions. Knowledge that is absolute removes erroneous ideas and illusions just as light banishes darkness.

When knowledge of your true nature and higher realities is flawless, your awareness will be clear, your perceptions will be accurate, your thoughts will be rational, your behaviors will be appropriate, and actions will produce desired results. When knowledge is flawed, your awareness may be blurred, perceptions may not be accurate, thoughts may be irrational, behaviors may not be ideal, and actions may not produce desired results.

Many people are satisfied to have enough knowledge of their true nature and higher realities to enable them to be only a little more comfortable, healthy, happy, prosperous, or successful. Truth seekers who are highly self-motivated to be spiritually awake cannot be satisfied with having ordinary states of mind and consciousness or the circumstances that correspond with them. They continue to learn and grow until their right endeavors and God's grace unveil and bring forth their innate qualities and capacities and they are fully Self- and God-realized.

Every mentally competent person has the capacity to elicit their innate spiritual qualities and wisely express them. What is needed is sincere desire to do it, and steadfast commitment to right endeavors, until the ultimate stage of spiritual growth is fully actualized.

The following story illustrates the kind of dedicated practice that allows ideal results to be experienced:

A disciple, approaching his teacher, asked, "Please tell me if I am progressing in the right way on the spiritual path."

The teacher responded, "Tell me what you have realized."

The disciple replied, "When I meditate, I am very peaceful.

My thoughts are subtle. The experience is very enjoyable."

"That's good!" the teacher affirmed. "But you haven't got it yet. Continue to practice."

After six months, the disciple reported: "Meditation is deep and long. I am often ecstatic. It seems that I am one with everything and I am overwhelmed with thoughts and feelings of unconditional love for everyone."

"That's good!" the teacher assured him. "But you haven't got it yet. Continue to practice."

Several months later, the disciple said: "Now, when I meditate, all thoughts are absent. There are no perceptions of otherness of any kind, only such exceptional clarity of awareness and wholeness that I cannot describe with mere words. After meditation, that clarity of awareness and wholeness continuously prevails."

"That's very good!" the teacher said. "Now you have it!"

You will know when your Self-realization is complete. Continue to practice until you have it.

You can more easily and quickly fulfill your ultimate purpose in life by doing what is necessary to allow your spiritual growth to naturally occur, while avoiding thoughts, feelings, and behaviors which do not enhance your life or clarify your awareness. By doing your utmost to allow spiritual growth to occur, you will have the support of evolutional influences; much evidence of God's grace in all of your wisely chosen, constructive endeavors; and continuous good fortune.

Answers to Questions About the Essence of Your Being and Relationship With the Infinite

How can I know which mental concepts I have about my true nature and my relationship with the Infinite are true?

If your concepts are compatible with what a spiritually enlightened person declares to be true, this might indicate that they are reliable. Only your own realization will satisfy you.

Can the full reality of God be known? Why don't more people know it?

It can be known by direct experience. It is not known by most people because they do not sincerely want to know it. They are satisfied with beliefs and opinions and prefer the company of others who think as they do.

What are some indications that our sense of relationship with the Infinite is real?

Some indications are: peace of mind; emotional stability; clarity of awareness; improved intellectual ability; a clearly defined sense of meaningful purpose for our lives; easy fulfillment of wholesome desires; a constant flow of necessary material resources, fortunate events, and circumstances; and satisfying, uninterrupted spiritual growth.

Regarding the four aims of life to have fulfilled: Do we have to live effectively, have wholesome desires easily fulfilled, and be continuously prosperous before being spiritually liberated?

Fulfilling the first three aims of life makes it easier to live freely and enjoyably, and nurture our spiritual growth. And the more spiritually aware we are, the easier it is to have the first three aims fulfilled. Effective living promotes spiritual growth and spiritual growth promotes total well-being.

I am an ordinary truth seeker who would be satisfied to have enough knowledge of higher realities to enable me to have a satisfying, trouble-free human existence. My personal circumstances are not pleasant. And it is not easy for me to imagine being Self- and God-realized.

Aim higher, and increase your capacity to accept all of the ideal circumstances that will enhance your life. For as long as you are satisfied to be ordinary, you will be inclined to have challenges and difficulties. Choose to be extraordinary and express excellence in all aspects of your life. Imagine how you will think and act, and what life will be like for you, when you are not confined by ordinary states of mind and consciousness. What you can imagine to be possible, and can believe to be real for you, can be actualized by your right actions and the support that the universe will provide for you.

How can we know that our spiritual path is right for us?

There is only one spiritual path: awakening from ordinary states of mind and consciousness to superconsciousness, Self-realization, God-realization, and liberation of consciousness.

Practices used to facilitate spiritual growth may differ. Do what produces the results you want to have. Avoid actions that are not productive. The practices that are common to all enlightenment traditions are disciplined thinking and actions; study of higher realities; contemplative meditation; and seeing through and rising above the mistaken sense of self. If you are affiliated with a formal religious tradition, while adhering to the outer rituals, attend to the basic practices that will enable you to awaken through the stages of spiritual growth.

I want to experience rapid, authentic, spiritual growth. To do this, is it necessary—or could it be helpful—to be a member of an organized religion?

Authentic spiritual growth is experienced when you do what is necessary to allow it to occur. It can be experienced with or without involvement with religious activities. Religious affiliation is a matter of personal choice. If teachings and practices are of real value, they can be used. If they are not of real value, they should be avoided. Doctrines that are not true should not be believed. Excessive association with small-minded adherents of erroneous religious doctrines will not contribute to your well-being or spiritual growth.

I am just beginning to sincerely study metaphysical principles and am a novice meditator. How long will it take for me to be able to comprehend higher realities and to experience obvious spiritual growth?

Your ability to comprehend higher realities and to grow spiritually will be determined by your capacity to learn and apply what is learned. Concentrated right endeavor will elicit ideal results. Indecisive, inattentive endeavor is not useful.

Investigate only the philosophical systems which are of value. Avoid useless metaphysical speculation. Test what is learned to verify its validity. Insightful investigation, verified by personal application, will result in positive, gratifying results.

Learn to meditate until you can easily be superconscious, then learn to be superconscious at all times while engaged in everyday activities. To meditate skillfully, first learn to relax and be mentally and emotionally calm. Observe changes in mental states and states of consciousness that occur when your breathing is slow and subtle. Use a meditation technique to improve concentration, then disregard it, and rest in the silence until your innate urge to have your awareness restored to wholeness is influential. Meditation will be satisfying and transformative. Be patient as you go forward with confidence.

How can I most beneficially integrate my duties and activities with my spiritual practices?

To integrate is to make into a whole by blending all parts together. Write a list of your duties and activities. Highlight those which are essential or important. Eliminate or minimize nonessential or unimportant duties and activities.

Put daily metaphysical study and meditation practice at the top of your list of essential activities.

Nurture your physical wellness with regular hours of rest and activity, appropriate exercise, and a wholesome diet (vegetarian is best for your health).

Fulfill your necessary or chosen social obligations without allowing distractions to cause you to neglect duties, metaphysical studies, or spiritual practices.

Be alert, decisive, and intentional. Think, feel, and act in ways which are for your highest good.

How can our innate desire to be spiritually awake be nurtured so that it can strongly, beneficially influence our life? Can we help others to be spiritually awake or is this a matter of their personal choice or destiny?

It can be nurtured by fervently wanting to be spiritually awake and assuming mental attitudes and lifestyle regimens that support that aim.

People who are interested in spirituality can be provided with helpful information that will enable them to help themselves. Your exemplary life can also inspire them.

Chapter 2

Sequential Categories, Specialized Capacities, and Orderly Processes of Cosmic Manifestation

Whether religious beliefs and the opinions of some scientists can be compatible is often vigorously debated. Proponents of orthodox religious doctrines may say that their intuition, or the revelations of saints or prophets of their tradition, provide all knowledge of the processes of life. While some scientists easily blend religious views with their knowledge of the laws of nature, many assert that God does not exist; that all of the processes of life can be understood by diligent observation of objective phenomena. Some scientists have suggested that if the "mind of God" could be known, a precise metaphysical and mathematical understanding of the universe, and all life, might be possible.

To bridge, or at least narrow, the gap between the views of intelligent religious thinkers, and scientists whose attitudes are materialistic but are willing to learn, accurate knowledge of the inner side of life will be helpful. Such knowledge will provide an explanation of a supreme Reality and its processes that can be seen as reliable when rationally investigated.

Not all readers for whom these concepts are new will immediately comprehend them. The most useful approach is to contemplate them in the light of reason and intuition, then allow your innate understanding to emerge in the course of time. At the innermost level of their being, every person has complete knowledge of the processes of life.

The Genesis (Origin and Beginnings)
of the Universe and Souls

One Reality produces and regulates objective phenomena. Its substratum (characterless substance that supports attributes of physical realities) is pure. Its two expressive polarity characteristics are its consciousness and power. The blending of its consciousness and its power produces a vibration (Om) from which all objective phenomena are produced. Subtle and gross material substances emerge from the consciousness of the one Reality. Consciousness is not produced from matter.

Three constituent (parts of a whole) attributes pervade the consciousness and emanated power of the one Reality and regulate the processes that occur in all realms or fields that it produces. A *field* is a region of space in which events occur, bounded or contained by a physical property such as gravitational or electromagnetic force. The Sanskrit word for each of the three constituent attributes is *guna*: an influence that is present when processes occur in a field.

Sattwa guna attracts, purifies, and illumines.

Rajas (activating influence) *guna* is transformative.

Tamas (darkness, inertia, heaviness) *guna* resists change.

The outflowing, vibrating power (Om), influenced by the purity of the one Reality produces a magnetized field of cosmic individuality. The positive polarity produces a cosmic intellectual capacity; the negative polarity produces cosmic mind.

The components of cosmic individuality—self-awareness, a sense of individual identity (cosmic ego), intellectual capacity, and a mind—are the same four characteristics which units of supreme Consciousness have when involved with fine, subtle, or gross fields of matter. Units which are not conscious of their pure essence of being are referred to as souls.

Five electric currents are projected from the field of cosmic individuality: one from the middle; one from each of the two extremities; and two from the gaps between the extremities. They form the cosmic causal field of supreme Consciousness.

The positive polarity of the cosmic causal field of supreme Consciousness produces five subtle essences of capacities of perception: touching, smelling, tasting, seeing, and hearing.

The neutralizing influence produces five essences of capacities of action: mobility, dexterity, utterance or speech, reproduction, and elimination.

The negative polarity produces five essences of gross matter: fine forces in space, air or gaseous substances, fiery or transformative influences, water, and gross substances.

The above fifteen manifestations of cosmic forces, with an intellectual capacity and a mind, form the most subtle material body of souls.

Sattwa guna produces fine matters in space. Sattwa guna with rajas guna produce gaseous substance. Rajas guna produces fiery or transformative influences. Rajas guna with tamas guna produce water. Tamas guna forms gross matter. Each kind of matter is said to have a minute part of the other four subtle element essences.

Biological processes of living things are governed by three element influences called *doshas*. Vata dosha, with space and air characteristics, influences movements and circulation. Pitta dosha, with fire and water characteristics, transforms. Kapha dosha, with water and earth characteristics, provides cohesiveness and stability.

The essence of being (sometimes referred to as the heart) which is aware, a sense of individual self-identity (ego), a faculty of intelligence, mind, fifteen subtle essences, and the five element influences that produce gross matter are the twenty-four principles of cosmic manifestation which emerge from the field of primordial nature.

Primordial nature is called *maya*: that which measures and

produces forms. In some philosophical systems it is called "the darkness" because it blurs the awareness of souls which are overly identified with it. Primordial nature, the substance of everything that is formed, is not an illusion. When sages say that the universe is not real, they mean that it will not exist forever. Tenacious attachment to objective phenomena results in suffering because events and circumstances are constantly changing.

The Eight Expressed Attributes of God

One expressed attribute of God is objective; seven are subjective. The one, objective attribute is cosmic individuality. It observes cosmic processes without participating in them, just as a person's sense of self-identity provides a viewpoint from which to observe what is perceived.

Six subjective attributes (three are pervasive, three are specialized) regulate the processes that occur in causal, astral, and physical fields. The seventh subjective attribute is God's all-pervading presence which is accessible to one who aspires to have a sense of relationship or communion with it.

Individualized units of pure consciousness produce their individual intellectual capacity, a mind, and causal and astral bodies as they become progressively involved with fields of objective nature. When they are incarnated, their life forces enliven their physical bodies.

Units of consciousness only identify with mental, causal, astral, or physical conditions. Their essence of being is not influenced by their perceptions or experiences. This is why awakening to Self-realization can suddenly occur when attention and awareness are removed from environmental influences and modified states of mind and consciousness. Self-realization is the restoration of one's awareness to its original, pure, wholeness.

The Seven Fields (Realms) of Cosmic Manifestation

The infinite, transcendental field beyond space and time is not influenced by the processes of cosmic manifestation. Only the expressive modes of supreme Consciousness produce and regulate objective forces in fine, subtle, and gross realms.

The seven fields that are produced by cosmic forces are:

1. The Cosmic Soul with three constituent attributes.
2. The Cosmic Soul's radiant, expansive field.
3. Primordial nature: the Om vibration in which space, time, and fine cosmic forces are unified.
4. Cosmic individuality, produced by the blending of the Cosmic Soul's radiant, expansive field with the field of primordial nature.
5. The causal field of magnetism, electricities, and causative essences with potential to manifest objective phenomena.
6. The astral field of life forces and energies.
7. The field of gross matter: the physical universe. There may be many space-time, physical universes.

The amount of energy pervading fine, subtle, and gross fields is constant; only its forms change. Energy radiations, all of which are forms of light, include cosmic rays, photons, gamma rays, x-rays, ultraviolet radiation, visible wavelengths, infrared radiation, microwaves, radio waves, and more.

Protons of atoms of gross matter have a positive charge, are stable, and have more mass than electrons which have a negative charge and are unstable. The energies of gross matters are held together by nuclear forces. Only a small portion of the energy in our universe is formed as gross matter. Most of it (called "dark matter") cannot be seen, though its gravitational influences are thought to have been detected.

The Five Sheaths That Cover & Veil Consciousness

When the essences of capacities of perception, action, and objects of perception are emanated, five sheaths or coverings of consciousness are produced. The first three sheaths form a soul's causal body.

1. A covering of fine matter through which the bliss (pure joy) of Self-awareness may be perceived.
2. The intellectual faculty.
3. The mind, which records perceptions and enables thinking and reasoning.
4. The astral sheath of energies and subtle essences of capacities of action.
5. The physical body, composed of material substances.

When subtle essences that can form a universe are emanated, the Cosmic Soul's superior power of attraction causes them to interact and a physical universe is produced.

When the power of attraction partially unveils the cosmic sheath of life force with capacities of action, vegetative life emerges on planets in solar systems that are stable enough to support it.

When the cosmic sheath with subtle essences of sensory capacities and powers of perception is unveiled, more complex life forms emerge and evolve.

When the cosmic mental sheath of aura-electricities which enables souls to use intellectual capacities is unveiled, human beings emerge on a planet and begin to evolve.

When a person's aspiration to be enlightened is supported by right living and right spiritual practice, the subtlest sheath which confines their awareness is unveiled and purified.

When Self-knowledge replaces one's mistaken sense of self-identity, consciousness is illumined.

When awareness is detached from modified states of mind and consciousness, one's true nature and the reality of God can be directly realized. When Self-realization is stable and flawless, liberation of consciousness is permanent. One is then impervious to all objective and subjective influences.

Several centuries ago, astronomers in India estimated the duration of our universe to be three trillion solar years. In 1894, Swami Sri Yukteswar, Paramahansa Yogananda's guru, published a small book, *The Holy Science.* He described how radiations from the center of our galaxy affect the mental capacities of human beings during ascending and descending subcycles as our sun and solar system moves in a 24,000 year orbit. As the sun moves toward the center of the galaxy, mental capacities of human beings become more highly developed. As the sun moves farther from the galactic center, mental capacities of human beings gradually diminish. Mental capacities of spiritually conscious people are not affected by external conditions.

Two 12,000-year cycles (one ascending and one descending) in a 24,000-year span of time. Each 12,000-year cycle have four eras (*yugas*). During a 1,200-year era, widespread mental confusion prevails. In the second (*dwapara*) era of 2,400 years, intellectual powers of human beings improve, enabling them to comprehend electric and magnetic properties in nature and to apply them for practical purposes. A third (*treta*) 3,600-year era emerges during which mental capacities become highly developed and people are able to comprehend the *source* of electric and magnetic forces. The fourth era of 4,800 years is *satya yuga*, during which the truth (Sanskrit *sat*) about higher realities is widely known. When this era has fully emerged, a descending 12,000-year cycle starts and human intellectual and spiritual capacities begin to gradually diminish.

As of 2007, 307 years of an ascending 2,400-year era of discovery and practical application of electric and magnetic proper-

SWAMI SRI YUKTESWAR

ties have passed. The third ascending era of increased mental capacities will begin in 4100. The fourth ascending era, of global spiritual enlightenment, will start to emerge in 7700.

Regardless of external conditions which may affect the circumstances of people who are not spiritually awake, individuals who choose to develop their intellectual, mental, and spiritual capacities can avoid being influenced by them.

There are now more people in the world who are able to comprehend the existence of subtle forces in nature and are adopting holistic lifestyle practices that can refine the physical body, improve mental and intellectual powers, and quicken authentic spiritual growth.

For many centuries, misguided "prophets" have made dire pronouncements of impending disaster for our planet and its inhabitants, or proclaimed that an era of enlightenment will soon occur. Such false ideas will continue to be promulgated until fantasies are no longer popular, and valid knowledge of evolutionary processes is more widely disseminated.

Insecure, dysfunctional people are often confused, afraid, and pessimistic. Self-confident people tend to be courageous, and habitually optimistic about near and distant future events and the improved planetary conditions that are yet to emerge.

In 1830 the global human population on our planet was one billion (a thousand million). A hundred years later, it was two billion. Forty-five years later (1975) it had doubled to four billion. Twenty-five years later (year 2000) it was six billion. At the present growth rate of approximately two hundred thousand new human incarnations daily, almost eighty million annually, another one billion will be added by 2010. If population growth continues at its current rate, by 2050 an estimated ten billion people will have to compete for food, water, and other natural resources that are necessary for their well-being.

Most of the population growth is now, and will continue to

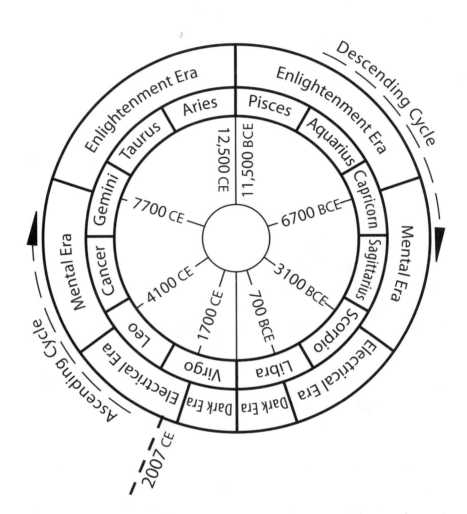

Progression of Cosmic Cycles

be, in undeveloped regions of the world where the quality of life is substandard. More than a billion people are existing on the equivalent of one dollar a day and at least that many do not have easy access to pure drinking water or sufficient food. Rapid population growth, pollution of the Earth's atmosphere because of widespread, inefficient use of fossil fuels and other causes, soil depletion, diminishing water reserves, imprudent cutting of forests, and the real possibility of continued global warming represent major challenges to the welfare of our planet and all forms of life. These are significant problems for which solutions can be found and implemented.

Of utmost importance is the spiritual education of receptive people of all ages throughout the world. When people lack knowledge of their true nature and their relationship to the whole, they tend to mistakenly presume themselves to be mortal, material creatures and are inclined to be egocentric, addicted to faulty opinions and destructive behaviors, and seldom concerned about the well-being of others or the environment. If they are religious without higher understanding, they may think that pressing problems can only be solved by divine intervention. They may hope for someone with superior wisdom and extraordinary powers to arrive on the scene, or a timely event to occur, that might adjust matters in their favor.

Paramahansa Yogananda sometimes referred to the trends of evolution that produce changes in nature and in human consciousness as expressions of "God's will." At an informal meeting with a few of his students, he said: "God's will, will be done, regardless of whether you cooperate with it or not. But how much better it is for you to cooperate! When you do, your spiritual growth is quickened and you can better serve others." He did not mean to imply that God is a cosmic person with wishes and intentions that ordinary people have. He was sharing insights about cosmic processes in a simple manner.

Sequential Categories & Emergence of Specialized
Capacities and Manifestations of Cosmic Forces

Pure Existence-Being (Supreme Consciousness)

The Cosmic Soul and Its Radiant, Expansive Field
with three constituent attributes: attracting, purifying,
and illuminating influence; transformative influence;
heaviness or inertia

Primordial Nature
Om vibration with time, space, and fine cosmic forces

blending of the purity of the radiant, expansive field
and primordial nature produces
Cosmic Individuality and Individualized Units (Souls)
with characteristics of:
awareness of what is perceived
self-sense (I-ness)
faculty of intellect
mind

Subtle Essences of Capacities of Perception
touch, smell, taste, hearing, and seeing

Subtle Essences of Capacities of Action
mobility, dexterity, utterance, reproduction, elimination

Subtle Essences of Elements
space with fine cosmic forces, air (gaseous substances),
fiery transformative influence, water (liquidity),
earth (cohesiveness)

Emergence of Gross Physical Matter
a universe and evolving forms of life

Answers to Questions About Categories and Processes of Cosmic Manifestation

Why are universes and souls produced?

They are produced because of the inherent inclination of supreme Consciousness to express, not because it needs to express in order to be improved or developed. The aspect of supreme Consciousness that is always pure-existence is not influenced by cosmic processes.

The processes of cosmic manifestation are not easy for me to understand. Is it necessary to fully understand them now?

It can be useful to examine them, from time to time, to have insights that will be meaningful. As your innate knowledge emerges, you will be able to see how it compares with these explanations and perhaps have them confirmed.

The processes of cosmic manifestation and how units of pure consciousness are individualized seems impersonal, unlike the traditional stories about God intentionally creating the world and caring about and having a plan for the salvation of souls.

The processes *are* impersonal due to the inherent inclination of supreme Consciousness to express. Souls awaken to liberation of consciousness gradually or quickly according to their degree of involvement with objective circumstances and their aspiration to be spiritually awake. By choosing to be influenced by elevating influences in nature and cultivating superconsciousness, awakening can be more rapid. That we can choose to be spiritually enlightened rather than try to believe a salvation theory propounded by others, whose ideas are personal opinions about the matter, should encourage us to assist ourselves to liberation of consciousness. Knowing our potential to be spiritually awake, we can choose to be awake.

Is there a stage of spiritual growth when our small sense of self-identity is relinquished in order to know our real Self?

For some people, the first obvious stage of awakening occurs when they are aware of being confined by their small sense of self-identity and are inclined to want to outgrow it. As their small sense of self-identity becomes weaker, they naturally become more aware of their true, changeless nature and are inspired to think and live without limitations.

If I am not fully Self-realized before I leave this world, can my spiritual progress continue in other realms, or will I have to reincarnate? What is it like in astral and causal realms?

Yes, spiritual awakening can continue in astral, causal, or realms beyond them—in the realm of primordial nature or in the Cosmic Soul's radiant, expansive field.

It is not necessary to consider reincarnation. For one who is intent on liberation of consciousness, reincarnation, if it is possible to do, and having to grow to physical maturity and adapt to mundane circumstances, is a waste of time.

Where one is after leaving the body is determined by their state of consciousness and where they can best continue their spiritual growth. The recommended way to leave the body is to do it while meditating superconsciously. Involvements with memories or subconscious influences can then be avoided.

Healthy, long, physical life has value because it provides opportunities to accomplish mundane purposes and to grow to emotional and spiritual maturity before leaving this world.

Astral and causal realms coexist with a physical universe. In astral realms, souls use mental and intellectual capacities while expressing through an astral body. Their experiences are in accord with their mental states and states of consciousness. In an astral realm, the circumstances of souls who are not spiritually conscious are usually similar to those which they had when they were incarnated. People who die in a confused mental state may continue to be confused for while. People who expect to "go to heaven" may have some mind-produced perceptions that are anticipated. Some souls may reincarnate very soon. Others may dwell in astral realms for hundreds or thousands of years, as time is calculated on earth, then either reincarnate or move to refined astral or causal realms.

In causal realms, souls express through a subtle, magnetic sheath and use mental, intellectual, and intuitive capacities. Because of the clarity of their awareness, their joyousness is constant. Not burdened with gross subconscious influences or sensual cravings, if they aspire to be fully awake they can more easily be Self- and God-realized.

While one is identified with a physical body, astral experiences are more common during dreams when awareness is removed from objective circumstances. It may also be possible to consciously use astral powers of intuition and clairvoyance and the more reliable, causal power of direct perception of what one desires to know.

All of the obstacles to spiritual growth can be removed or transcended while incarnated.

Chapter 3

The Psychological and Physiological
Basis of Spiritual Enlightenment

Rational thinking, emotional maturity, and adherence to life-style regimens that nurture physical and psychological health provide a firm foundation on which authentic, spiritual growth can be actualized.

Holistic Living Nurtures Complete Psychological and Physiological Well-Being

To acknowledge all components of life as parts of a whole and have them harmoniously blended is to live holistically. The *psyche* is the "soul" that energizes the mind and enlivens the body. Modern *psychology* includes the study of mental processes, emotions, and behaviors of individuals or groups of individuals. *Physiological* processes are normal functions of physical organs and systems.

How to Think Rationally and Be Emotionally Stable

The way to think rationally and be emotionally stable is to be Self-aware while dispassionately viewing the contents of the mind and outer events without being unduly influenced by them. When you are Self-aware, you can be serenely discerning. When you are not Self-aware, your attention may be inclined to identify with the contents of your mind and external events.

The mind is disordered, blurred, and fragmented by influences that modify it. Five such influences, which may be of two kinds, are: 1) knowledge of what was or is observed; 2) illusions, inaccurate perceptions of what was or is observed; 3) hallucinations or fantasies, perceptions which are not based on facts; 4) sleep states with or without dreams; 5) memories which are not objectively viewed. These influences may be troublesome, painful, confining, or restrictive, or may not be troublesome, painful, confining, or restrictive.

If your acquired knowledge is valid, wisely use it. Avoid illusions and fantasies. Learn to sleep without allowing your awareness to be dulled or your powers of discriminative intelligence to be impaired. Observe memories as mental impressions of prior perceptions without allowing them to interfere with rational thinking or emotional serenity.

Some common symptoms of mental distress are sadness, anxiety, emotional unrest, restlessness, and irregular breathing. Avoid these conditions by discerning the difference between yourself as the observer and what you observe, and by meditating to the stage of superconsciousness which removes your awareness from modifying influences.

The immediate way to remove troublesome mental and emotional states is to *replace them with mental and emotional states which are more desirable*. This can be done by decisively changing your mental attitude and by performing constructive actions which enhance your life. Cultivate the positive habits of being cheerful, optimistic, self-confident, self-reliant, and thankful for the good fortune that you have had, and now have. To be self-reliant is to think and act from the core of your being, knowing that you are supported and provided for by the Reality in which you abide.

If thoughts, memories, or events that occur elicit feelings of sadness, regret, grief, guilt, resentment, frustration, anger, fear, or other painful thoughts and emotions, refuse to allow them to prevail. Replace sadness with inner joy; regret, with resolve to behave appropriately and make wiser choices; grief, with understanding; guilt, with self-forgiveness and resolve to behave better; resentment, with forgiveness of others and insightful analysis of unpleasant situations; frustration, with feelings of freedom; anger, with peace of mind; and fear, with courage and self-confidence. Constructive thoughts, feelings, and actions weaken and remove troublesome subconscious influences. The power to live victoriously is within you.

Use will power to discipline thoughts and feelings and develop powers of concentration. Your thoughts will be better organized and your emotions will be more stable when your lifestyle routines are well-ordered. Adhere to regular schedules of restful sleep, purposeful activity, meals, appropriate physical exercise, study of higher realities, and meditation practice. An erratic lifestyle will result in mental confusion, lethargy, low energy reserves, and emotional unrest.

One debilitating effect of mental confusion is the inability to discern what is true. Many people think they are physical beings, cannot comprehend higher realities, and believe that physical demise will be the permanent end of their existence. That is why they may feel hopeless and helpless—and may be inclined to grasp at, or cling to, material things, relationships, and circumstances.

Wisely choose your friends and social relationships. Avoid allowing what others say or do to disturb your inner peace. Established in Self-awareness, speak and act appropriately. Be calmly observant and discerning. Concentrating on useful purposes will make it easier to live as you want to live.

An effective way to control mental and emotional states and states of consciousness is to control how you talk. Avoid frivolous, useless talking. Monitor the thoughts that wander through your mind which may unduly influence your states of consciousness, moods, or behaviors.

Be Willing to Grow to Emotional Maturity

When you were a child, still learning to adapt to others and your environment, it was normal to sometimes feel dependent, insecure, and confused. As an adult, it should be normal for you to be self-reliant and know your relationship with the Infinite. Many emotionally immature people who say they are religious, or are truth seekers, are inclined to want an infantile relationship with God—to want God to love and care for them as their parents, and perhaps others, did. If they sincerely want to experience spiritual growth, they have to outgrow their emotional dependency, discard childish ideas, and acquire accurate knowledge of higher realities that will enable them to be self-reliant and responsible for their actions and experiences.

When your thoughts or emotions are conflicted, or your behaviors are undisciplined, immediately identify with your essence of being and think, feel, and act from that awareness of Self-knowing. By living effectively in this world, you will be able to live effectively wherever you are in the near or distant future. Because the wholeness of the Reality of God is present where you are, you can consciously know it, harmoniously relate to it, and always have its constant support.

Refine Your Nervous System and Fully Develop the Capacities of Your Brain

Until the late 1900s, most of the information about soul-mind-body relationships was provided by individuals who spoke or wrote about their personal experiences and insights. Very little was known about how states of mind and consciousness influence the brain and other physical processes.

When the nervous system is overstressed, the immune system is weakened and debilitating changes in body chemistry can occur. It has been estimated that 60 percent of the problems that people ask physicians to help them resolve are stress-related. Some of their symptoms may be anxiety, mild or moderate depression, high blood pressure, frustration, anger, confusion, heartbeat irregularities, tiredness, apathy, insomnia, erratic behaviors, and feelings of helplessness and hopelessness.

Studies indicate that mental abilities and brain capacities can be improved through the years. The human brain reaches its maximum weight of about 3 pounds when a person is 20 years of age, then slowly starts shrinking. By age 50, memory formation usually slows down. By age 70, approximately 12 percent of the population have various degrees of cognitive impairment, indicated by frequent short-term memory lapses, and may be more likely than their peers to have Alzheimer's symptoms.

For decades, researchers thought that little could be done when brain capacities started to diminish. In the early 1970s, it was discovered that the brain remains "plastic" throughout one's life and, with training, new skills can be learned. It has been observed that people who "exercise" their mind and brain by doing simple, rapid math problems and doing things that require alertness, concentration, and adaptability, greatly improve their mental abilities. Being creative and innovative when performing daily tasks and acquiring new skills can also be helpful.

Meditation, practiced for at least twenty minutes once or twice a day to elicit physical relaxation and mental and emotional calmness, is now often recommended by medical doctors for their patient-clients who need to learn to manage stress. A simple meditation routine, which can be easily learned and used, causes a decrease in metabolism, breathing rate, heart rate, and blood pressure. A word, or short phrase, is used as a mantra to focus attention and elicit the positive responses.

Several recent studies by neuroscientists, using proficient meditators as subjects, a brain-scanning device for observing patterns of blood flows in the brain, and biofeedback instruments to record brain wave patterns, have provided interesting information. When the mind is calm and awareness is clear during a meditation session, the prefrontal lobes of the brain are active. The prefrontal lobes of proficient meditators are more developed than those of people who have not regularly meditated. In one study, of women who were about fifty-five years of age and had similar lifestyle circumstances, long-term meditators were biologically younger than others in the group who did not meditate.

Some meditators who were mentally calm later reported that, while meditating, they were not aware of any boundaries in relationship to space, time, and environmental conditions; they were aware only of a sense of infinite oneness. Brain scans indicated that areas in the upper, back region of both hemispheres of the brain that enable a person to relate to ordinary perceptions of space, time, and environmental conditions, were quiet because they were not processing any sensory input.

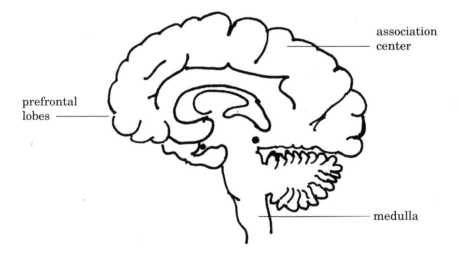

Stimulation of brain centers or the absence of stimulation, also seems to be related to some of the unusual perceptions that have been reported by people after having what seemed to be a near-death or out-of-body experience.

Some commonly reported perceptions are:

1. It is ineffable (cannot be fully described).
2. Mental and emotional calmness.
3. Perceptions of sounds.
4. Seeing a tunnel of light, and going into it.
5. Going into a realm of bright light.
6. Sensing a benevolent *presence*.
7. Meeting and communicating with others.
8. Reviewing major events of one's life.

These experiences cannot be adequately described to people who have not had similar experiences, because they are subjective: occurring within one's mind and consciousness.

Mental and emotional calmness and a sense of detachment are commonly experienced when attention is inward and brain centers which process sensory input are quiet.

Sounds that may be heard are usually produced in the mind by activated brain centers. Various sound-frequencies of the Om vibration may also be heard.

The tunnel, which seems to attract one to enter into it, may be dark or may be a radiant, gold color.

A realm of bright light is often felt to be where one truly belongs, as though one has returned to their source. It is also said that a sense of an all-pervading, benevolent *presence* provides feelings of comfort and reassurance. And what seems to be direct access to vast realms of knowledge is said to reveal the reality of God, the processes of the universe, and the real meaning of life.

Deceased friends or relatives may appear and verbal or telepathic communication may seem to occur. What seem to be spiritually enlightened beings are seen and sometimes provide instruction. A religious person may see saints or other role models about whom they had prior knowledge. Devout Christians may see Jesus. Hindus may see Krishna. Some say they saw God as God is. Much of the information that seems to be communicated and is felt to be meaningful, is not always clearly remembered after returning to ordinary awareness. A common experience of people who had a near-death episode is of being told by someone, or by an inner voice, that they had to return to body consciousness and attend to their mundane duties for several more years.

Near-death life-review perceptions occur when memories are elicited by brain stimulation. Such perceptions may also be had when one is awake while experiencing a life-threatening event: a traumatic automobile accident, falling from a ladder, almost drowning, or being physically attacked.

After returning to ordinary consciousness many people said they were inclined to be more intentional and purposeful in their choices of lifestyle activities and behaviors, and more kind and thoughtful in personal relationships.

Many near-death episode perceptions are similar to those which may be experienced during deep meditation when one's attention is internalized and awareness is removed from outer conditions. Sounds may be heard, a tunnel of light may be seen, and brilliant lights of various colors may appear. When the sound of Om is heard, it can be meditatively contemplated. When the tunnel is seen, one can go through it to the bright light. When a meditator discerns that perceptions are brain-produced, they should be transcended because they are distractions from the ultimate aim of meditation practice.

Out-of-body perceptions may occur during twilight sleep, when one is extremely tired or overstressed, physical safety is threatened, or when in a semiconscious state undergoing a surgical procedure. I have had meditative perceptions similar to those that are described by persons who experienced near-death events and sensations of being out of my body.

In 1951, during a Sunday afternoon, I was meditating in the chapel of the Self-Realization Fellowship Center in Phoenix, Arizona, where I was the associate minister. The sudden noise of a nearby door being forcibly closed interrupted my concentration. As I again turned my attention inward, suddenly, I was point of awareness in a vast, dark blue, infinite space with small, sparkling white lights in the distance. A few moments later, I returned to ordinary consciousness.

Two out-of-body sensations occurred spontaneously. The first one was experienced in Orlando, Florida, two days after President John F. Kennedy was assassinated in Dallas, Texas. While in Orlando to present a lecture, I was a guest in the home of friends. While resting on the bed during the early afternoon, not yet asleep, I could hear people talking in the adjoining room. Suddenly, I seemed to float upwards. When I was near the ceiling of the room, I turned over, looked down, and saw my body on the bed. A moment later, I descended and blended with my body. For a few hours after that experience I felt a mild, aching sensation at the base of my skull.

The second out-of-body sensation unexpectedly occurred a few years later, in San Francisco. On a bed, in a hotel room, just before drifting into sleep, I felt a mild pressure at the base of my skull. A thought came into my mind: "I wonder if I can withdraw from my body?" Deciding to experiment, I mentally "pushed" against the back of my head and seemed to move a short distance behind my body, then went forward and again identified with it.

As the nervous system becomes refined and the capacities of the brain become fully developed, mental abilities improve, intellectual powers are enhanced, and spiritual growth occurs spontaneously. Since your consciousness is processed through your brain and nervous system while you are incarnated, do all that you can do to be as healthy and functional as possible.

In the kriya yoga tradition which I represent, it is said that the capacity of the brain to process cosmic conscious states is naturally increased by diseaseless living, psychological well-being, good nutrition, fresh air, sunlight, and wholesome environmental conditions. Aspiration to be spiritually awake that is supported by attentive superconscious meditation practice refines the nervous system and improves the brain's capacities to process refined states of consciousness. Instead of experiencing gradual transformative changes in the course of time, it is possible, with concentrated practice, to accomplish in a few years what might otherwise require many decades of ordinary physical evolution.

Dedicated meditators can be taught a unique pranayama technique with which they can circulate life force through the spine and brain to refine the nervous system and prepare it to accommodate clear states of consciousness. Their spiritual progress can then be greatly accelerated.

The Seven Astral Centers In Your Spine and Brain

Life forces in these astral centers (*chakras*) enliven your physical body and regulate its functions. Your states of mind and consciousness can also be related to their influences.

A soul's life force enters the physical body at the medulla oblongata, at the base of the brain, and flows down the spine. From the lower region of the spine it provides energies that express through the chakras. Dormant life force (*kundalini*) in the body may be aroused by compassionate thoughts and feelings, fervent aspiration to be spiritually conscious, devotional prayer, meditation practice, the influences of a pure environment, and personal, spiritual, or mental contact with a person in whom vital forces are freely expressive.

The three channels (*nadis*) in the astral spine are: the central channel (*sushumna*, the radiant path); one on the left side (*ida*), a cooling or calming influence; one on the right side (*pingala*), which is heating or stimulating.

When flows of life force are dominant in the left channel, it is easier to be calm and think rationally. Dominant flows in the right channel may stimulate the mind and emotions; this is not a useful influence when you want to be calm, but can be useful when you want to achieve goals or complete projects. When life force flows primarily in the central channel, interactions between the hemispheres of the brain are more coordinated, and meditation is easier. This is why it is useful, when you sit to meditate, to be aware in the spine, then move your awareness upwards to the front and higher regions of the brain.

There is a direct relationship between flows of life force in the channels in the spine, and right and left nostril breathing dominance. When physiological and psychological conditions are normal, right nostril breathing is dominant for about two hours, followed by left nostril breathing dominance for about two hours. During right nostril breathing, flows of life force are more forceful in the right channel; when breathing through the left nostril, flows of life are more forceful in the left channel. During the intervals between nostril-breathing dominance, when flows of life force in the channels are balanced, mental and emotional states are inclined to be calm.

You can use a simple method to balance the flows of life force in both channels when you want to be mentally and emotionally calm, especially just before starting to meditate.

- Sit upright. Inhale deeply. Exhale. Relax.
- With a finger, close the right nostril. Inhale smoothly through the left nostril. Pause for a moment.
- Close the left nostril and exhale smoothly through the right nostril. Pause for a moment.
- Inhale through the right nostril. Pause. Exhale through the

left nostril.
- Do this ten consecutive times. Then inhale deeply, exhale and relax. Notice that you are more calm and centered.

In the following descriptions of characteristics related to the seven chakras, the tastes, colors, and sounds are produced by their unique life force (*prana*) frequencies. The tastes may be experienced in the throat and mouth; the colors and sounds may be perceived when one is meditating. These colors and sounds are mentioned in ancient yoga texts.

- First chakra, at the base of the spine has the earth element attribute. The taste is sweet. The color is yellow. The sound is as the buzzing of bees. Sanskrit *muladhara*, "foundation." Characteristic influences are mental and emotional stability.
- Second chakra, at the sacral region of the spine. Water element. The taste is astringent. The color is white. The sound is like that of a flute. Sanskrit *swadhisthana*, "abode of ordinary self-consciousness." A common characteristic is sensualness.
- Third chakra, at the lumbar region of the spine opposite the navel. Fire element. The taste is bitter. The color is red. The sound is like that of a harp. Sanskrit *manipura*, "the city of gems." When awareness is related to this chakra, one may have self-control and fervent aspiration to spiritual growth.
- Fourth chakra, at the dorsal region of the spine between the shoulder blades. Air element. The taste is sour. The color is blue. The sound is like a continuous peal of a gong. Sanskrit *anahata*, "unstruck sound." When identified here, one has mastery of the senses and life forces.
- Fifth chakra, at the cervical region of the spine, opposite the throat. Space element. The taste is pungent. The color is gray or misty with sparkling points of white light. The sound is like an ocean's roar. Sanskrit *vishudda*, "pure." When awareness is identified here, one may have exceptional powers of intel-

cerebrum
crown chakra

prefrontal lobes
spiritual eye

cervical chakra

dorsal chakra

lumbar chakra

sacral chakra

base chakra

lectual and intuitive discernment.

- Sixth chakra, between the eyebrows, the spiritual eye center associated with the front lobes of the brain. Life forces flowing upward and focused here may be perceived as a dark blue orb with a golden halo and a silver-white light in a field of blue. Gold color is said to represent the energy-frequency of Om; dark blue, the frequency of all-pervading Consciousness within creation; the white, star-like light is of Consciousness beyond relative phenomena. Sanskrit *ajna*: command or control; decisive power of will.
- Seventh chakra, related, but not confined, to the higher brain. Related to pure consciousness, transcendence of mental and physical states and all conditions that modify or distort awareness. Sanskrit *sahasrara*, "thousand rayed."

The Unveiling and Actualization of Innate Qualities and Capacities and Progressive Awakenings Through the Stages of Authentic Spiritual Growth

Self-realization is not a condition to be attained; it is your natural state of being to be consciously experienced.

When a soul is fully identified with a mind and body, it is inclined to think that it is a physical being. When it becomes aware of itself in relationship to a mind and body, it can know that, as an observer, it is not that which is observed. Knowing this distinction can be a first stage of Self-discovery.

As a partially conscious soul's innate capacities are unveiled by the power of attraction of its essential purity and its innate urge to be fully conscious, it becomes more aware and assumes an illusional sense of self-identity. Though its consciousness is modified and somewhat confined, it can use its mind to think and use its functional capacities to accomplish useful purposes. Most people in our world are at this stage of soul awakening: conscious enough to relate to, and express in, the physical world while not yet, or perhaps only dimly, aware of higher realities. As their intellectual and intuitive powers improve and their awareness is clarified and expanded, they will begin to be more superconscious.

Refined superconscious states enable awakening souls to apprehend their true essence as a unit of a larger Reality. They may then be inclined to investigate the subtle principles and processes that express and support objective phenomena and aspire to be completely Self-knowing. At this stage, they can choose to discipline thoughts and behaviors, and engage in practices which nurture their psychological transformation and elicit their innate qualities and functional capacities. They can then experience superconscious states (which may first be modified by disordered mental and emotional influences), pure superconsciousness, and states of cosmic consciousness that provide complete knowledge of one Reality and its expressive modes.

To Experience Easier and Faster Spiritual Awakening, Remove All Obstacles That Interfere With It

The primary obstacle to spiritual awakening is the flawed perception of one's essence of being. Instead of thinking and acting as a mere physical creature, decisively think and act as the immortal, spiritual being you are. Don't allow yourself to be limited by an illusional sense of self or by modified states of mind and consciousness. Instead of wasting time and effort endeavoring to overcome nonuseful habits of thinking and behaving, discard them. Concentrate your attention and actions on matters which enhance your life.

Until your spiritual growth is spontaneously progressive, constantly aspire to be spiritually awake. Sustained aspiration and an optimistic mental outlook will attract a constant flow of favorable events that will provide opportunities to grow to emotional and spiritual maturity.

Answers to Questions About the Psychological and Physiological Basis of Spiritual Enlightenment

How can our ability to make right choices and think rationally be improved?

Write a list of goals that you want to achieve and the other things you want to do that will be satisfying and of real value. Write what you will decisively do about these matters. When you know what you want to achieve, and will do, you will be able to think rationally, make the right choices, and perform productive actions. While imagining possibilities, be realistic and practical. As you proceed with your plans and projects, your self-confidence and functional abilities will improve.

I can usually view memories with objectivity. At other times, I become emotional and confused, especially when remembering unpleasant events or the mistakes I have made. What are some ways to avoid emotionalism and confusion?

When you are too mentally and emotionally involved with memories, remind yourself that, as a spiritual being, you can choose not to be influenced by memories.

Breathe deeply a few times to relax your body and release unpleasant feelings. Take a brisk walk or perform an exercise routine that will make you breathe more deeply and cause the brain to release chemicals that will help you feel better. Walking leisurely can be helpful, especially if you look at the passing scenery and stay aware in the moment.

How soon can negative thoughts and feelings be permanently replaced with constructive thoughts and feelings?

They will be immediately changed when you decide to change them. Allowing negative thoughts and feelings to prevail is a self-defeating habit that should be discarded. Life is enjoyable and satisfying when thoughts and feelings are positive. Choose to be happy and optimistic.

I have an intellectual understanding of what God is. Now and then, I tend to revert to thinking about God as a cosmic person and am inclined to want to have a personal relationship with God who cares for me, will help me, and will reveal himself to me when I am receptive.

Many people think like this because they feel dependent or haven't yet discarded some of the false ideas they acquired when their thinking was traditional. Or they have friends who talk about God as a person. A concept of Reality that enables you to have a sense of relationship with it can be helpful until actual realization of it emerges. As your awareness is clarified, intuition will provide direct knowledge of what God is.

Is it possible to be Self-and God-realized without first being psychologically healthy and having a refined nervous system and fully developed brain capacities?

It is possible to have episodes of transcendence of ordinary states of mind and consciousness that allow glimpses of higher realities to be had. To sustain superconsciousness, it is helpful to have a refined nervous system and more fully developed brain capacities. While attending to useful spiritual practices, nurture your psychological and physical well-being. Become more aware of your astral body. Feel your life forces flowing in the spine and throughout the body. Positive psychological and physical changes will more quickly occur.

Can kundalini energies awaken spontaneously?

Yes. When the innate urge to be spiritually awake becomes influential, dormant forces can be aroused that will begin to flow upward through the astral channels in the spine. Identification with the physical body and the mistaken sense of self (ego) is then not as confining. Intellectual and intuitive powers improve. The body is vitalized. Metaphysical concepts are more easily understood. Meditation is easier to practice. Spiritual growth is progressively faster. Lifestyle preferences may change. Goals, activities, and relationships that were considered to be important may no longer be appealing. Consciousness expands. Small-minded inclinations are outgrown or easily renounced.

It is best to allow transformative changes to occur rather than to resist them or try to understand them from an egocentric point of view. To tenaciously cling to nonuseful modes of thinking and behaving as innate qualities and capacities are being unveiled, can cause mental confusion and interfere with the awareness-clarifying, soul-liberating process.

> One who is without sentimental attachments, who does
> not [overly] rejoice when circumstances are pleasant or feel
> [strong] aversion toward that which is unpleasant, is
> firmly established in understanding.
> – *The Bhagavad Gita 2:57*

Chapter 4

Superconscious Meditation Practice That Clarifies Awareness and Facilitates Authentic Spiritual Growth

Withdrawing attention from environmental circumstances and mental states allows superconsciousness to be experienced. To become proficient in eliciting superconscious states, all that is required is regular, skillful meditation practice and being alert and attentive at other times.

Superconsciousness is to be *elicited*: *allowed* to come forth, rather than be thought of as a state of consciousness that can be produced by personal effort. Superconsciousness is also referred to as the fourth state of consciousness because it is other than, and superior to, the ordinary awake state, dream state, and unconsciousness during deep sleep.

Eliciting superconsciousness is important because it is the stage beyond modified states of consciousness from which further awakening to Self- and God-realization can occur. Many people who want to be Self- and God-realized cannot awaken to the stage of enlightenment (spiritual knowing) because they have not learned to rise above ordinary states of consciousness which confine them to an egocentric point of view. When they renounce or transcend the mistaken sense of self and are able to be superconscious, they will be receptive to the emergence of Self- and God-consciousness. The degree of clarity of a person's awareness determines their capacity to be spiritually conscious and freely functional.

How to Practice Superconscious Meditation

If you are already superconsciously meditating on a regular schedule, continue to practice. If your meditations are not satisfying, experiment with some of the following methods until you discover the process that provides satisfying results. If you are not yet meditating on a regular schedule, resolve to do it.

- Practice once or twice a day. Early morning meditation will enable you to be poised and to more skillfully perform your duties during the day. Late afternoon or early evening meditation will reduce stress that may have accumulated during the day, calm your mind, and settle your emotions.
- If you are learning to meditate, do it for at least 20 minutes to allow enough time to relax and be peaceful. If you are a more experienced meditator, adhere to your usual routine.
- Any quiet place where you will not be distracted is suitable. Having a special place in your home that is used only for your meditations can be helpful. When you are there, it may easier to detach your attention from thoughts of mundane concerns. If having a small altar, with pictures of saints or spiritual role models, helps you to focus on your purpose for being in that special place, have one. Have some inspirational books or other spiritually oriented literature readily available.

A Simple Meditation Routine

- Sit upright in a comfortable chair. Sitting on the floor, or on a bed or couch, is all right if you are comfortable.
- Close your eyes. Inhale deeply. Exhale, and feel relaxed. Do this two or three times.
- Open your mind and your heart (being) to the Infinite.
- Put your attention and awareness in the front and upper regions of your brain. Avoid effort; just "be there."
- Use a meditation technique to elicit physical relaxation, calm

your mind, and focus your attention.
- When a meditation technique is no longer needed, discard it.
- Rest in the clear state of awareness for a while. This stage of practice is most beneficial; superconscious influences can then purify your mind and enliven and vitalize your body.
- Conclude the session.

Before concluding the session, acknowledge that everyone in the universe and all souls in other realms are in the wholeness of God, as you are. Wish for their highest good.

Avoid worry or concern about your progress. Results will soon be evident. Exceptional meditative experiences are not necessary. The mental peacefulness, emotional stability, clarity of awareness, improved powers of concentration, physical well-being, and a more obvious sense of being in harmony with the rhythms of life that you will have, are obvious indications that your meditation practice is beneficial.

Avoid allowing subjective perceptions to distract you from the purpose of practice—which is to be proficient in eliciting superconsciousness. Preoccupation with ecstatic physical or emotional states (which may be produced by fervent prayer, pranayama, devotional chanting, or mental imagery) is a form of autoerotism: self-gratification of desire to experience intense pleasurable sensations. Go beyond transitory, subjective perceptions. Aspire to experience only the pure joyousness of Self-knowing.

Avoid talking about your spiritual aspirations, practices, or meditative experiences with others—except with your mentor or spiritual adviser, if you have one.

Be self-motivated to meditate, alone, on a regular schedule. Occasional meditation with compatible friends can be helpful. The superconsciousness of proficient meditators may elevate and clarify the awareness of the other participants.

Avoid dependence on others. Improve your understanding of your true nature and your relationship with the Infinite by regular superconscious meditation practice, rational thinking, and adherence to holistic living regimens. Do everything that you know to do to be fully, spiritually awake and to bring forth and express your innate, divine qualities and capacities.

Three Effective Meditation Techniques

A meditation technique is a procedure that can be used to calm your mind and detach your attention from thoughts and feelings that interfere with concentration.

- *Pray.* Audibly or mentally pray to be spiritually awake, then sit quietly, waiting and observing, allowing your innate urge to be spiritually awake to determine your experience.
- *Use a mantra*: *God*, *Om*, *peace*, or any word that is comfortable for you. With your attention and awareness in the front or higher region of the brain (or both places), mentally repeat the word. If your attention wanders, gently bring it back to your point of focus. When your body is relaxed, breathing is slower and your mind is calm, let the mantra fade away and sit in the silence.

   Or use a two-word mantra. Examples: *Om-God*, or one of the Sanskrit mantras, *so-hum* or *hong-saw*. Mentally speak the first word as you inhale, and the second word as you exhale. Let your breathing be natural. As you relax and are mentally calm, disregard your breathing and continue to mentally recite the mantra until your attention is focused, then let the mantra fade away and sit in silence for a while.
- *Meditate in Om.* Listen in both ears and around your head until you hear a subtle sound frequency. When you hear it, try to hear a subtle sound behind it. Continue to do this until the sound that is heard doesn't change and is constant. Consider that sound to be a characteristic of the vibration of Om. Identify with it and expand in it. Feel that you are one with Om

while contemplating its source: the radiant field of the Cosmic Soul. Then contemplate the field of absolute existence-being.

Use the technique that enables you to meditate most effectively. Experiment until you discover what is most helpful for your purposes. If you meditate more than 20 minutes, when you are aware that your attention is not focused or you are too passive, use intention to be alert and focused, pray, use your mantra, or meditate in Om. When silently sitting, keep your attention and awareness in the front and/or higher region of your brain. Patiently sit until you are peaceful and your awareness is clear.

Stages of Meditative Superconsciousness

By attentive observation, you will be able to determine the degree of clarity of your superconscious experiences.

- Preliminary superconsciousness may be mixed with modified states of consciousness, random thoughts, memories, and emotions that interfere with concentration.
- Refined superconsciousness may be mixed with subtle influences of modified states of consciousness, thoughts, and emotions which are easier to disregard or transcend. If they are not transcended, they may produce subjective phenomena: sensations of expanding; floating, or moving in space; visions of people or places; or what seem to be insights or revelations which, when remembered, are not significant.
- Pure superconsciousness is devoid of mental and emotional influences. When meditating, if subliminal influences are not completely quieted, they may occasionally activate thoughts and feelings which interrupt concentration.

Realizations of Oneness*

*The Sanskrit word for oneness is *samadhi*, "the bringing together completely" of attention and awareness with a meditative object.

There are three kinds of oneness-realization:

- *Complete identification of attention and awareness with a meditative object of contemplation: sound, light, joy, feeling that one is free in space, or whatever was contemplated.* This oneness is supported by an object of perception. While it can be helpful because it keeps subliminal influences pacified, it does not liberate consciousness. Some meditators are only able to experience this stage of oneness because they do not aspire to go beyond it.
- *Meditative, Self-knowing oneness detached from objects of perception.* A superior realization with accurate knowledge of one's true essence of being and higher realities.
- *Constant Self-knowing oneness while thinking, relating to others, and performing effective actions.* When this realization is permanent, liberation of consciousness is certain.

Meditative contemplation is practiced by looking at something with keen expectation of having knowledge of it or being one with it. To have knowledge about the processes of cosmic manifestation, the essence of your being, or the truth about God, acknowledge what you already know while hopefully wanting to know more. To be one with Om and with God, let your awareness be *almost* absorbed in Om, then go beyond it to merge your awareness in God. To experience the pure-conscious essence of your being, sustain your aspiration to do it while withdrawing your awareness from emotions and thoughts. If at first you are not successful, persist. Aspiration and diligent, right endeavor will eventually enable you to have the results you want to have. By experimenting with meditative processes to verify their practical usefulness, you will soon be a proficient meditator. Exploring subjective realms and higher realities is completely different from being habitually, outwardly directed as most people are. When you are knowledgeable about the inner side of life, you will be able to live more freely in the mundane realm.

How to Always Be Superconscious

Learn to be fully alert when you are meditating and to stay alert after meditation practice. While engaged in activities and relationships, be Self-aware and cultivate peace of mind and emotional stability. Adhere to holistic lifestyle regimens. Avoid provincial (small-minded) mental attitudes and behaviors: judgmental attitudes and comments; gossip; excessive curiosity regarding the private behaviors and circumstances of friends and neighbors; rigid personal, political, or traditional religious opinions; and feelings of superiority or pride regarding racial, ethnic, or family history, social status, or personal accomplishments.

You cannot be superconscious, or Self- and God-realized, while allowing provincial, personality-oriented attitudes to influence your thoughts, feelings, and behaviors. Choose to be spiritually awake. Demonstrate firm resolve by renouncing all Self-limiting mental attitudes and behaviors and rising above ordinary states of mind and consciousness.

Being always happy, optimistic, healthy, mentally peaceful, emotionally stable, creatively functional, and prosperous indicates that your spiritual growth is authentic. If you are unhappy, pessimistic, have frequent physical problems or mental or emotional conflicts, have difficulty doing what you want to do, or lack necessary material resources, bring forth your innate, divine qualities and express them. You are not in this world to merely survive while hoping for conditions to improve or to eventually be Self- and God-realized. Your current incarnation is your opportunity to cultivate and use extraordinary powers of perception and exceptional abilities to freely live as you are meant to live and to fully awaken to Self- and God-realization. If you are not doing this, your sojourn in this world will be neither satisfying nor of spiritual value.

Millions of people are born, wander through space and time as though in a dream, and die without seriously thinking about their relationship with the Infinite or doing anything to know it. Not yet aware of their potential to be spiritually awake, they waste most of their mental powers and vital forces in useless endeavors and temporary satisfaction of meaningless desires.

Imagine the events, circumstances, and relationships that will be for your highest good and either create or attract them. Use your knowledge and skills to accomplish what you want to accomplish. If you have meaningful aims and purposes that seem too difficult for you to accomplish, let the universe help you to accomplish them. Meditate until you are calm and aware of your oneness with the wholeness of life. Before concluding a meditation session, think about how you want your life to be and float your hopes and desires in the Om vibration until you feel fulfilled. You will be inspired with creative ideas, energized, and empowered to perform actions that produce ideal results.

Answers to Questions About
Superconscious Meditation Practice

I am a novice meditator. What should I first learn to do?

For four to six weeks, sit for 20 minutes once or twice a day
to relax and experience a clear state of awareness. When this is
easy to do, if you want to sit longer, do so. Stay alert and attentive. Twenty minutes of alert meditation is more beneficial than
longer, passive sessions.

Is meditation a form of hypnosis?

No. Superconscious meditation elevates awareness beyond
ordinary conscious and subconscious states. Using hypnosis to
modify or reprogram subconscious levels of the mind is not spiritually beneficial.

Are some meditation techniques more effective than others?

Any method that enables you to quiet the mind and almost
effortlessly concentrate is suitable to use. When a technique is
no longer needed, it can be discarded. Many meditators, who are
able to immediately experience a clear state of awareness, may
use a technique later during their practice session if they need
to refocus their attention.

When I meditate, and my mind is very quiet, I sometimes see a
tunnel of gold (or dark blue) light. What should I do with it?

You can experiment with it. If your attention is attracted to
it, allow yourself to have the sensation of being pulled into it.
The experience is subjective. Dispassionately observe what occurs and is perceived. It may be an opportunity to have your
consciousness expanded and to experience what it is like to have
a self-view that is much different from your ordinary sense of

self. After having an unusual meditative perception, when the session is concluded, be fully aware in the moment. Avoid being otherworldly or indulging in fantasics.

I think I experience a state of oneness when I meditate. When I come out of meditation, I don't clearly remember how it was when I was absorbed in that state. It doesn't seem to provide me with insights or enable me to be more alert and Self-knowing.

You are probably experiencing a subconscious-oneness. An authentic conscious-oneness (samadhi) leaves an impression or memory in the mind that can be accessed. While it does not always provide insights into higher realities, it usually has an awareness-clarifying effect that is apparent after having had the experience.

It is not easy for me to meditate. Is it really necessary to do it to be superconscious?

Meditation is recommended because it is a way to withdraw awareness from mental and emotional influences which interfere with concentration. You can be superconscious in the midst of activities by being alertly attentive and using your meditation-acquired ability to withdraw attention from troublesome mental and emotional influences. You will discover that you can choose to think only constructive thoughts and be free from debilitating feelings such as grief, anger, resentment, and frustration.

What can I do to stay alert when I meditate? When I relax, I am inclined to either go to sleep or into a borderline sleep state.

Have enough restful sleep. If you are still inclined to go into a subconscious state when meditating, remained poised, open your eyes, and look straight ahead without focusing on anything. Keep your eyes steady. Notice that you are centered and focused. After sitting like this for a while, close your eyes and stay alert.

When I first sit to meditate, I am not always as intentional and inspired as I would like to be. What can be done about this?

Remind yourself that your meditation practice session is an opportunity to be spiritually awake. Having a small altar with a picture of a saint or items that arouse devotional feelings may be helpful. Reading a few verses of scripture or inspired words from some other literary work, quiet chanting, or praying can also support your intention to deeply meditate.

My desire to be Self-realized and to experience the full reality of God is sometimes so intense that I become frustrated and unhappy because of my lack of spiritual progress. What can I do to have peace of mind and be more emotionally stable?

I understand your concern. During my first year with Paramahansa Yogananda, after I had been meditating for several months, I was occasionally discouraged because of the seeming slowness of my spiritual growth. In a private conversation, he said to me, "You have to want to know God with all of your heart, but you have to be patient until you do."

Desire to be God-realized should be balanced with patience, which can soon be acquired by nurturing soul-contentment in all circumstances. While being patient, don't be satisfied with existing conditions that are not in accord with your highest aspirations to be spiritually awake and freely functional. It will be helpful to integrate your spiritual practices with your personal duties and activities. Use your creative abilities to live skillfully now rather than wait until you are Self- and God-realized. Your spiritual awakening will be faster.

The key to effective application of the law of attraction is to believe that you have what you need or want, rather than wait until results are forthcoming before you will believe. Constant attunement with the Infinite and unwavering faith allow the law to flawlessly work. As with all laws of cause and effect, the law of attraction operates when you cooperate with it.

Declare With Conviction

Knowing that I am one with the Infinite, I firmly believe that everything for my highest good is always easily provided for me.

Don't just stand at the sidelines of life passively observing what other people are doing. Have your own learning and growing experiences. First learn what works and what doesn't work, then proceed with keen interest regarding the outcome. Anticipate the near and distant future good fortune that you will have while being soul-centered and thankful for the good fortune that you have in the moment. By being thankful for the good fortune you now have, you will attract more of it. Sustained thoughts and feelings of having what you need or want attract it. Thoughts and feelings of not having what you need or want repel it.

I don't experience oneness or have exceptional perceptions or insights when I meditate, though I am calm and peaceful. Does meditating like this contribute to my spiritual growth?

Yes. Maintaining mental and emotional calmness after you meditate will allow your spiritual awakening to spontaneously occur. You will be more alert and intellectually and intuitively discerning. Sudden insights into higher realities and the meaning of life will emerge into your awareness. You will become more cosmic conscious: knowing that one Reality is appearing as all of the things, life-forms, and processes in the universe.

I am satisfied with my spiritual growth progress. My health is good, my circumstances are comfortable, and I have a surplus of financial resources. I feel inclined to do something of value for others. What are some things I can do?

Continue to nurture your spiritual growth. Decide how to use your knowledge, abilities, and material resources to do the most good. Avoid excessive emotional involvement, working too hard, or depleting your financial reserves. If you have a large surplus of money, give some of it to organized endeavors that are doing good work. In a will, specifically describe how you want the remainder of your estate to be used when you are no longer here. Your thoughtful choices will continue to benefit others far into the future.

Chapter 5

Guidelines to Dedicated Discipleship

Every person who wants to experience rapid spiritual growth that culminates in liberation of consciousness must be firmly committed to discipleship. To be assisted and encouraged on the discipleship path, having the wise guidance of a competent teacher (guru) can be helpful. Hearing about the facts of life, learning spiritual practices, and having a teacher as a guide and role model, will not produce optimum results if what is learned is not effectively applied. With or without a teacher, discipleship is experiential: only actions that produce psychological transformation can allow spiritual growth to easily occur and innate Self-knowledge to be unveiled.

Spiritual growth is the spontaneous emergence of innate capacities which, in many people, are confined and restricted by ordinary, modified states of mind and consciousness. There is a need to acquire higher knowledge and purify the ego, mind, and consciousness to allow these capacities to be actualized.

Complacent satisfaction with existing circumstances, and allowing thoughts, moods, and behaviors to be influenced by non-useful habits, subconscious tendencies, or the words or actions of others who are similarly inclined, are common obstacles to spiritual growth. For discipleship to be of value, a radical examination of thoughts, feelings, behaviors, and other conditions that interfere with spiritual growth is necessary. Constructive changes of mental attitudes and behaviors along with intentional performance of effective actions will enable you to experience faster spiritual growth.

Situations and Relationships to Avoid

- *Teachers whose behaviors are not conformed to what they teach.* While a teacher who does not *live* what he or she teaches may be able to provide valid knowledge, it is better to have a teacher whose personal example is ideal. What is taught will then have greater influence because it will be transmitted with the authority of personal experience and the nonverbal sharing of the teacher's mental states, states of consciousness, and spiritual forces.
- *Cultishness.* Obsessive devotion to, or extreme involvement in, religious practices or activities based on rigid beliefs or endeavors to control thoughts and behaviors of adherents rather than encourage self-reliant behaviors that nurture emotional maturity and authentic spiritual growth.
- *Circumstances or personal relationships that complicate your life or distract you from your highest aims.* Simplicity and purposefulness are essential for one who is dedicated to the spiritual path. Circumstances and relationships that are not yet ideal can be patiently endured until they are improved or changed. The key to being patient, when it is necessary to endure temporary discomfort or unpleasant circumstances is to cultivate soul-contentment. When outer conditions are not yet ideal, by being calm and peaceful you will avoid mental or emotional unrest while performing duties and nurturing your spiritual growth.

To think that you can be peaceful only when external circumstances and personal relationships are ideal, is to live precariously. Circumstances and personal relationships are certain to change. The way to have constant peace of mind and wellbeing is to be established in flawless Self-knowing while calmly viewing transitory conditions as they come and go.

Spiritual teachers may play one or more of the following roles according to their abilities and capacities:

- *The reminder,* who shares valid information, explains metaphysical principles, and helps disciples reclaim their pure-conscious essence of being. The disciple's innate knowledge of higher realities is elicited and satisfying spiritual growth can be experienced.
- *The awakener,* who is at least partially Self-realized, whose spiritual energies can be transmitted to disciples to arouse their dormant soul forces.
- *The bestower of liberation,* who guides and assists disciples to awaken through the stages of spiritual growth to Self- and God-realization that liberates their consciousness.

The Necessary Characteristics and Capacities of a Person Who Wants to Be a Disciple

If you do not yet have the following characteristics and capacities, acquire them. Examine your mental attitudes and behaviors and make the necessary changes. The characteristics and capacities that a disciple should have are:

- *Sincere interest in learning.* While acquiring knowledge of higher realities and improving functional skills, discard the erroneous ideas that interfere with rational thinking, effective living, and spiritual growth.
- *Sufficient intellectual capacity to learn.* If your interest in learning is sincere, your powers of intellectual discernment can be improved. Discern the meaning of spoken words and the intention behind them. Attune your mind to the mind of the authors of written words; endeavor to know what they knew when they wrote their thoughts.

When I was with Paramahansa Yogananda, I carefully listened to what he said, was attentive when he was silent, observed his demeanor, and attuned my mind and consciousness to his. To disciples, he said, "I am pleased when you understand what I say. I am even more pleased when you understand without my having to say it."

- *Willingness to use what is learned.* Acquired knowledge is powerless unless it is wisely used. When it is possible to do so, test what you learn to verify its validity and usefulness. Knowledge will then be of practical value. You will become skillfully proficient with practice.

- *Absence of mental perversity:* intentional or habitual deviation from what is right or appropriate. It inclines a person to distort useful information for self-serving purposes to maintain an egocentric condition and avoid having to change their nonuseful modes of thinking and behavior. A characteristic of egotism is an unrealistic, inflated sense of self-importance or competence.

- *Respect for what is taught.* When it is true and helpful, it should be respected. If it is not true, it can be disregarded. A competent spiritual teacher will teach only what is true and of value.

- *Respect for the teacher.* Courteous, honest communication with one's spiritual teacher allows knowledge to be easily transmitted. Mental and spiritual attunement enables the disciple to receive nonverbal knowledge from the teacher's illumined mind and consciousness.

A teacher's primary purpose is to educate, encourage, and assist disciples to rise above their mistaken sense of self by using their intellectual, intuitive, and functional abilities.

How to Be a Dedicated Disciple On the Spiritual Path

The spiritual path can be enjoyable.

- *Discipline your thinking, feelings, and behaviors.* Think constructively. Be emotionally calm and Self-reliant. Adhere to wholesome lifestyle regimens and live in harmony with the rhythms of nature. Be compassionate, moral, ethical, and honest in personal relationships. Allow your actions to be directed by the life-enhancing impulses that arise from the core of your being rather than passively allowing them to be determined by habits, moods, irrational ideas, or the words or actions of others whose views and behaviors are incompatible with yours. What you do or experience that enhances your life, continue doing or allow to occur. What disturbs your peace of mind or does not contribute to your overall well-being, avoid.

- *Live with a clear sense of meaningful purpose.* While you are incarnated, there are necessary duties to perform and useful purposes to accomplish. Your primary duty is to nurture your spiritual growth until you are Self- and God-realized. Live holistically: harmoniously integrate all aspects of your life while performing actions which allow your spiritual growth to most easily occur.

- *Profoundly study metaphysical (higher) realities.* Regularly do this to nourish your mind with positive ideas and improve your understanding of your spiritual nature and your relationship with the wholeness of life.

- *Intensively engage in spiritual practices.* Spiritual practice is intensive when constructive actions are concentrated. Besides superconscious meditation practice, let how you think, feel, work, relate to others, and nurture the environment be your spiritual practice.

- *Cultivate a conscious relationship with God.* You can partially know God by using your intellect; more accurately know God by intuitive perception; and completely know God when you are Self- and God-realized. Cultivate constant awareness of the omnipresent reality of God at all times, and your sense of communion with the presence of God will soon blossom as complete realization.

Dedicated discipleship will permanently free you from the conditions that formerly clouded your mind and confined your awareness. Your mental states and states of consciousness influence your thoughts, emotions, actions, experiences, and circumstances. Mastery of attention that you acquire will improve your powers of concentration and enable you to more accurately discern the truth of what you observe. The constructive influences of superconscious states elicited by skillful practice of meditation will purify your mind and clarify your awareness. You do not have to be confined and limited by ordinary states of mind and consciousness during your sojourn in this world.

Until liberation of consciousness is complete, the ultimate Reality may be thought of as a presence with which to enjoyably commune rather than knowing that one is a unit of it. Communion can provide a sense of being anchored in the Infinite, purify the mind, and regenerate the body. For as long as there is a sense of being separate from God, even though a sense of relationship exists, continued contemplation of the reality of God is needed until God-realization is constant.

Glimpses of Self- and God-knowing may be had during early stages of spiritual awakening. With sustained aspiration and concentrated endeavor, Self- and God-knowing will prevail during interludes of superconscious meditation and when you are engaged in ordinary activities and relationships.

Dedicated discipleship will empower you to remove or rise above all obstacles to spiritual growth and quickly fulfill your spiritual destiny.

Affirm (Emphatically Declare) With Self-Confident Intention
Fully committed to spiritual discipleship, my thoughts and
actions are always in accord with my resolute decisions.
The complete Self- and God-realization to which I aspire,
I compassionately wish for everyone, everywhere.

Answers to Questions About Dedicated Discipleship

How can a competent, reliable spiritual teacher be found?

Instead of looking for such a teacher, prepare yourself for discipleship. When you are ready to learn, and to apply what is learned, if you need a teacher, you will meet the right one. A reliable spiritual teacher will encourage you to test the guidelines that are given to prove their value for yourself. Always be realistic; avoid fantasy. Avoid teachers or organizations that advertise their methods as being a fast way to enlightenment.

An enlightened spiritual teacher cannot do your work for you. Even though you learn the facts of life, holistic lifestyle regimens, and beneficial spiritual practices, and perhaps have life forces aroused, you will still have to do the necessary things that allow psychological transformation.

If you are sufficiently intelligent and fully committed to your spiritual path, a teacher may not be necessary. Information can be acquired from books and other reliable sources, and a course of disciplined endeavor can be chosen that will enable you to awaken through the stages of spiritual growth.

It is important to be willing to outgrow emotionally immature ways of thinking and behaving, cultivate self-confidence, and improve your intellectual and intuitive powers.

The aim of being Self- and God-realized seems too high for me to believe to be possible in my present incarnation.

You have to live your life. Why not do it the way you know to be best? Avoid thinking that discipleship is difficult. There is always the possibility that you will have sudden insights and quickly awaken to Self- and God-realization.

Chapter 6

Three Transformative
Practices to Effectively Use

Your mind can be calm. Your thoughts can be rational. Your awareness can be clear. Your consciousness can be illumined. All of your personal circumstances and relationships can be harmonious and satisfying. Knowledge of how these ideal conditions can be experienced is available and you can use it.

Why are many people who read metaphysical literature and are involved in various self-help systems not as healthy, happy, spiritually conscious, and skillfully functional as they say they want to be? The answer: They do not effectively use the information they acquire. They may say "the processes don't work for me" or "maybe I'm not meant to accomplish anything worthwhile." The real problem is their inclination to want results without having to change their thinking, feeling, or behaviors.

Why are some people happy, healthy, and prosperous while others are not? People who are always happy, healthy, and prosperous consider their circumstances to be normal. The differences between people are their mental states and states of consciousness. A self-confident, self-motivated person can accomplish what is imagined and believed to be possible. People who are insecure and confused tend to allow themselves to experience the effects of their negative self-image, erratic thinking, and dysfunctional behaviors. They see themselves as victims of circumstances over which they have little or no power to control.

If you are not yet fully expressing your innate potential to be freely functional, apply the following spiritual practices.

The Transformative Results of Positive Affirmation*

*Latin *affirmare*, to strengthen. To declare to be true.

Observe your thoughts and conversations. Do you always think and declare what you want to be true for you, or do you think and declare lack and limitation? Are you self-confident? Are you optimistic? What are you producing or attracting that corresponds with your thoughts and spoken words?

If you need to cultivate habits of positive thinking, feeling, speaking, and action, use concise, clearly defined affirmations to declare the experiences and circumstances you need or desire to be yours now. Whatever you really need or want, first possess it in your mind and consciousness and it can be yours in fact.

- Know what you need or want. Be specific. Do you need or want improved health, a comfortable abode, a better job, success in a business venture, more money, peace of mind, spiritual awareness, freedom from bad habits or addictions?
- When you know what you need or want, decide to have it. Don't think about why you should not, or cannot, have it.
- Declare that you have it. You can have peace of mind immediately. Physical health and spiritual awareness will progressively improve. Outer changes can occur quickly.

Write a concise affirmation that clearly defines what you need, want, or already have and want to continue to have.

Example:

> I am spiritually aware, mentally peaceful,
> emotionally stable, physically healthy,
> abundantly prosperous, have ideal personal
> relationships and circumstances, and always
> thrive and flourish in all aspects of my life.

Speak the affirmation aloud, with conviction, until thoughts and feelings to the contrary cease. Immediately assume (take on) the mental attitude, feeling, and state of consciousness that you declare to be yours.

There is no magic or mystery involved when using affirmations. Simply declare that you have what you need or want. Allow your unwavering faith to constructively influence your thinking, feelings, and decisive actions while being receptive to the unplanned good fortune that life can and will provide for you.

Constructively Use Creative Imagination*

*A mental picture or concept of a thing, event, situation, or circumstance. Creative imagining is intentional or controlled.

Mentally picture and feel that what you need or want is already accomplished.

- Sit still until your mind and emotions are calm.
- Vividly imagine the end results of what you need or want to experience. Know and feel, at the deepest level of your being, that you have what you need or want.
- Sustain that conviction and feeling after the session.

Do what you know to do to have it. If you don't know what to do, sustain the conviction and feeling of accomplishment and allow life to provide supportive events that will bring what you imagine into manifestation.

Forty years ago, I knew a man who used imagination to be successful in a business venture. Two years later, some of his managers left the company and created a similar business, taking with them several skilled employees. Instead of using his imagination and personal skills to attract new, competent, trustworthy people, he allowed himself to become depressed and resentful, used alcohol to escape from reality, and let his business fail. Many years later, when I met him again, he was still impoverished and constantly talking about how he had been betrayed. Even though he knew what to do to change his circumstances, he allowed his thoughts, moods, and behaviors to be unduly influenced by his feelings of resentment.

If the experiences and circumstances that you imagine are not always actualized, avoid thinking that you cannot succeed. Persist until you are successful. Learn by participating in the creative process. With practice, you will acquire proficiency in using your imagination to produce ideal outcomes. The clearly defined needs or desires that you picture in your mind will be impressed into cosmic mind, which will cause events to occur and circumstances to unfold that will result in fulfillment.

When using creative imagination, forceful endeavor is not needed. Define your needs and desires; gently intend for them to be fulfilled. Know and feel that they are fulfilled. Use creative imagination to "see" and "feel" yourself to be spiritually enlightened. How will you then think, feel, and act? What will you do? What will be your understanding of your true nature and your relationship with the Infinite?

Behind the outer appearances of the physical realm are invisible forces that regulate the processes of life. Learn to be aware of them. Invite them to be supportive of you and they will be supportive in accord with your receptivity to your highest good. Know and feel that you are fulfilled. Thoughts and feelings of unworthiness tend to attract corresponding events. As an immortal, spiritual being, choose to be spiritually conscious, happy, healthy, and successful in all of your meaningful endeavors.

How to Pray* Effectively

*Latin *precari*, to obtain by entreaty or earnest request. To make such a request. Reverent petitioning of God for something desired or needed.

Motivation that inspires one to pray may range from desire for material benefit to hope of union with God.

Prayer style may be vocal, mental, or wordless aspiration.

Some common forms of prayer include: acknowledgment of the good fortune one already has, thanksgiving, confession, asking for help, and intercession for others who need help.

Contemplative prayer is simple, surrendered awareness of God's presence without words or concepts. When a sense of communion is not felt, patiently sit with knowledge that God is real. The more conscious you are of abiding in God, the less inclined you will be to ask for anything. When awareness of your relationship with God is constant, supportive events and circumstances will effortlessly emerge.

God is the cosmic unit of supreme Consciousness; you are an individualized unit expressing through a mind and physical body. Knowing this, rather than praying *to* God, pray *in* God. Before praying, clearly define your needs and desires. To do this, it may be helpful to write them. A good time to pray is after an interlude of meditation when you are calm and rational.

- Be still until your mind is calm and you are aware of being one with God. If you cannot immediately be aware of the reality of God, acknowledge that you are *in* God.
- Don't beg for what is needed or wanted. Acknowledge that you have it. Claim it by feeling, at the deepest level of your being, that it is already yours.
- Rest for a while in that consciousness of fulfillment until you are permanently established in it. Know, at the core of your being, that you are one with the wholeness of God.
- Be thankful that you have that realization (experience with knowledge) of fulfillment.

If you pray aloud, or mentally, continue to the stage of silent contemplation of your relationship with the Infinite, then to the stage of recognition and joyful acceptance of fulfillment.

When praying for others, pray for their highest good to be realized rather than try to cause specific outcomes to occur.

It can be helpful to have a written account of your creative imaginings and prayer practices, and the results that follow. This will help you to define what you need or want and to be confident as your endeavors produce beneficial results.

The Positive Results of Your Clearly Defined
Creative Imaginings and Prayers

Write these procedures in a notebook or private journal. Your awareness of your relationship with the Infinite will improve and you will be increasingly self-confident and successful.

What you needed or wanted:

_____

When you imagined or prayed for it to be actualized: _____
The positive results:

_____

What you needed or wanted:

_____

When you imagined or prayed for it to be actualized: _____
The positive results:

_____

What you needed or wanted:

_____

When you imagined or prayed for it to be actualized: _____
The positive results:

_____

What you needed or wanted:

_____

When you imagined or prayed for it to be actualized: _____
The positive results:

_____

Affirm With Conviction
Always conscious of my relationship with the Infinite,
I joyously accept the complete fulfillment that is available
to me now. This realization of wholeness that I have,
I compassionately wish for everyone, everywhere.

Answers to Questions About the Three Supplemental Spiritual Practices to Effectively Use

How often should an affirmation be used?

When the desired changes of mental attitude, feeling, and consciousness are definitely experienced, affirmations are no longer necessary.

It is difficult for me to form a mental picture of ideal events or circumstances. What else can I do?

Feel the fulfillment, satisfaction, and happiness you will have when the events and circumstances actually exist.

To what form or aspect of God should I address my prayers? Would it be helpful for me to pray to a saint?

You can pray to the omnipresent, formless Reality or to God as you imagine or experience God to be. Regardless of the form or aspect of God that is invoked, you are always in relationship with the Source. If you pray to saints or spiritual role models who are no longer in this world, even though they do not hear you, your concept of such a person may be a "point of contact" with the Source. Pray *in* God until you know and feel that what you pray for is a present reality.

Chapter 7

Infinite Life

Infinite life is without boundaries or limits. If your life is not yet like this, creatively imagine how you will think and act, and what your circumstances will be, when your life *is* like this.

Anticipating what is possible to experience will empower you to live effectively, see opportunities that you could not see before, and attract events and circumstances that are for your highest good in all aspects of your life. Your highest good prevails when you are spiritually awake; mentally alert and rational; emotionally stable; physically healthy; satisfied in relationships that are harmonious and supportive; easily able to have the material resources you need; and living enjoyably and successfully with a clear sense of meaningful purpose.

Understand and Coordinate the Relationships Between Your Subjective States and Objective Circumstances

Thoughts and feelings are subjective. What is outwardly observed and experienced is the objective reality. By carefully examining your states of consciousness, mental and emotional states, and personal circumstances, you will be able to discern their corresponding relationships. Assume states of consciousness and nurture thoughts and feelings that will constructively influence your actions and produce or attract ideal events and circumstances.

Allowing outer events or circumstances to adversely influence your mind and consciousness will result in mental and emotional confusion and interfere with your endeavors to be freely expressive. Avoid thinking that other people or circumstances can prevent you from bringing forth your potential to be fully awake and skillfully functional.

Infinite life will be natural and easy when you are always established in Self-knowledge and know that you abide in the wholeness of one Reality that has within it everything that you need for your total well-being.

Until you are able to always, effortlessly be in the flow of supportive events and circumstances, use your knowledge and skills to live effectively while nurturing your spiritual growth.

Write a list of your real needs. Examples: increased spiritual awareness; improved intellectual powers; healing or improved health; a comfortable place to live; a job or a better job; more money; satisfying personal relationships; necessary material things; and other real needs.

Write a list of what you want to have and what you want to do or accomplish. Beside each entry, explain why.

Examine your thoughts and feelings about what you have written. Are you aware of thoughts or feelings of resistance to having what you need or want, of not being able to have them, or of unworthiness? Renounce those thoughts and feelings.

If you need more knowledge and special skills to have your needs satisfied and your wants fulfilled, acquire the knowledge and use it; acquire the skills and use them. Be receptive to the unplanned good fortune that you can have when you are in tune with the Power that enlivens and nurtures the universe.

After having done the best of which you are capable, if you do not have the results you need or want, or have to confront situations which you cannot resolve, avoid anxiety about those matters. Direct your attention to the Source; rely on it to provide for you and to resolve discordant or unpleasant situations.

The more conscious you are of the omnipresent Reality in which you abide, the easier it will be for you to know that all you need for your complete well-being is available to you. You will not have to ask for anything or use a lot of effort to accomplish your inspired purposes. You will live with graceful ease in harmonious accord with the rhythms of life. Memories of past unpleasant experiences will not influence your mind or awareness. All present-time events and circumstances will be in divine order. Your near and distant future experiences will be meaningful and enjoyable.

Having permanently transcended ordinary states of mind and consciousness, you will effortlessly continue to awaken to complete Self-realization and liberation of consciousness.

Answers to Questions About Infinite Life

Is infinite life really possible in the world as it is today, with so much strife and many confused and suffering people?

Yes, it is possible for anyone, anywhere, who is conscious of their true nature in relationship to the Infinite, regardless of the conditions that are experienced by others who are not spiritually aware. To help others, compassionately bless them with your thoughts of good will while you are living effectively and awakening to Self-realization. Your illumined consciousness and exemplary life will benefit everyone.

I have thoughts and feelings of resistance to having what I need and want, of not being able to have them, and feelings of unworthiness. It is not easy for me to let go of these thoughts and feelings. What can I do about this?

Replace troublesome thoughts and feelings with thoughts and feelings of self-worth and openness to the good fortune that is always available to you—and you deserve to have. Be self-reliant, self-confident, and purposeful. Bring forth and fully actualize the potential that is within you to experience excellence in all aspects of your life.

Isn't it a form of escapism, or denial of facts that exist, for me to remove my attention from troubles and direct it to the Source?

Being in tune with the Source while accomplishing your purposes is the ideal way to live. If you have done the best of which you are capable without having positive results, or are confronting situations you cannot resolve, complete reliance on the Source will allow it to do for you what you could not do. You will not have the mental and emotional unrest, anxiety, or feelings of despair which interfere with your ability to function effectively and be in the flow of supportive events.

Meditate in thought-free silence until you are conscious of your oneness with the wholeness of life. After meditation, be receptive to the guidance that will emerge from within you and to the opportunities that are available for your total well-being. When you see, or hear about, others who are thriving, be happy for them. Learn to expect, see, and easily accept the blessings that you can have.

Past experiences are history: events which cannot be changed. Your future experiences, in this world and beyond, will be determined by your states of consciousness and actions. Knowing that you are an immortal, spiritual being, live freely now.

Guidelines to Holistic Living

holistic Emphasizing the importance of the whole and the interdependence of its parts.

Live joyously, creatively, and effectively by harmoniously integrating the spiritual, mental, emotional, physical, and environmental components of your life.

Begin each day with thoughts of God and your relationship with the wholeness of life. Meditate 20 minutes or until you are peacefully established in Self-awareness.

Attend to duties efficiently. Focus attention and actions only on matters which are important.

Exercise regularly. Maintain ideal body weight. Choose a diet of nutrition-rich foods. A vegetarian diet is best for health.

Manage material resources wisely. Pay bills on time. Avoid long-term debt. Wisely invest a portion of your income for your future financial security and personal needs.

Be cheerful and optimistic. Expect the best possible outcome for every emerging situation.

Use imagination to produce ideal circumstances and attract favorable events, resources, and personal relationships that are for your highest good and the highest good of others.

Think thoughts and do things that will enhance your life and nurture your spiritual growth.

Silently acknowledge the innate, divine nature of every person and relate to them with respect and kindness.

Constantly aspire to be fully, spiritually awake.

Affirm With Conviction

Fully aware of my relationship with the wholeness of life,
I choose to live wisely, joyously, creatively, and effectively.
The freedom I have, I compassionately wish for everyone.

Addendum

The Evolution of Religious Beliefs and Practices

Although humans have been on our planet for many thousands of years, their history is little known. It is believed that early civilizations, indicated by self-governing groups of people who provided for themselves by cultivating food crops and domesticating animals, were established approximately fourteen thousand years ago in Egypt in the lower Nile River region and in the lower half of Iraq. Organized groups were also formed in Africa, India, China, and other regions of Asia.

Prior to the beginnings of civilizations and of what are now considered as major world religions, diverse beliefs regarding a divine or supernatural power prevailed among tribal groups in various regions of the world. Some groups in the southern region of Russia, who called themselves Aryans (honorable or noble people), are now known as Indo-Europeans because their language was the basis of several European languages. They imagined the forces of nature and conditions which determined human affairs to be influenced by higher powers to which they offered sacrifices of various foods and animals. In the middle of the third millennium before the current era, some of them traveled to what is now Scandinavia, Germany, Greece, Italy, and northern India. In the course of time, they became two separate groups speaking different forms of Indo-European, one form being Sanskrit, which is still used today. The religious beliefs and practices which were eventually formalized continued to evolve, and often strongly influenced human cultural development as well as political decisions.

1800 – 1500 BCE
Judaism: Babylonia, Israel, Lebanon

The name Judaism is from Judah, the fourth son of Jacob, the son of Abraham, founder of the Hebrew people. The word Jew is from Latin *Judaeus*, from Hebrew *Yehudhi*. Doctrines of Judaism are in the Torah: the first five books of the Old Testament. Monotheism (the teaching that there is only one God) is the basis of Jewish idealism and religious practices.

You shall love your neighbor as yourself. – *Leviticus 19:18*

Hinduism: India

The name that best describes the cultural customs and religious views and practices of the majority of the people of India is *Sanatana Dharma*, "the eternal way of righteousness." Dharma means "that which upholds or supports."

The name *Hinduism* was coined by foreigners. The river Sindhu, forming a part of the western boundary of India, was pronounced as *Hindu* by ancient Persians, changed to *Indu* by the Greeks, and later changed to English *Indus*. The Greeks called the country east of the river, India. Its people became known as Hindus and their beliefs and practices as Hinduism. Contrary to popular belief, a variety of gods is not worshipped; one supreme Reality is acknowledged. The so-called "gods" are viewed as expressive forces and powers of that Reality. The philosophical concepts and practices of adherents of Sanatana Dharma as described in the Vedas, considered to be "revealed knowledge," are more fully expounded in an extensive body of literature, of which the Upanishads and the Bhagavad Gita are most widely known.

Lead me from the unreal to the real; lead me from
darkness to light; lead me from death to immortality.
– *Brihadaranyaka Upanishad*

600 to 500 BCE
Shinto (the "teachings" or "way of the gods"): Japan

Shinto evolved from prehistoric religious traditions. It now has influences of Buddhism and Confucianism. Some of its features are a strong sense of family lineage, social cooperation, and emphasis on reverence for one's ancestors.

In ancient times, Shinto priests were members of special hereditary clans or ritual families which served the court. Today, large shrines utilize full-time priests; smaller shrines are served by part-time priests. A priest's general role is to mediate between the gods or spiritual forces (*kami*) and the local populace, and to present offerings.

Confucianism: China

Confucius (*K'ung Fu-tsu*, "great master K'ung") taught that every person's destiny is determined by benevolent behaviors.

According to tradition, he was a government worker in the federal state of Lu. At about age fifty, aware that his superiors were indifferent to his ideals, he quit his job and for thirteen years traveled from state to state, hoping to initiate social and political reform, before settling down to write. He taught that to bring order and peace to the world, people should learn to live in accord with their virtuous tendencies.

Hold faithfulness and sincerity as first principles. – *Confucius*

Buddhism: India

Named for Buddha, a title indicating that a person is considered to be spiritually enlightened: from the Sanskrit verbal root *budh*, "to be fully awake, to know."

Siddhartha Gautama, a young Indian prince, was sad when he saw the suffering that most people experienced. Wanting to discover the permanent solution to the problem of human suffering, he left home, examined various philosophical systems, and learned and practiced yogic meditation methods. After devoting several years to ascetic lifestyle regimens that made his body weak and did not enhance his awareness, he chose the "middle way" of moderation. His ultimate aim, which he realized, was *nirvana*: the complete cessation of conditions which confine awareness and interfere with one's endeavors to be Self-knowing.

A core-teaching of Buddhism is that strong desires which cause mental and emotional distress, and incline one to act unwisely, should be renounced or overcome by practicing the tenets set forth in the eightfold path. Its categories are: moral conduct (right speech, right action, right livelihood); mental discipline (right endeavor, right mindfulness, right concentration); and intuitive wisdom (right views, right intentions).

Speech, actions, and livelihood should be constructive and supportive of the welfare of others. Endeavors should be wisely motivated and effectively executed. To be alert and see things as they are is to be mindful. Concentration results in mastery of attention. Intuitive wisdom provides accurate knowledge of oneself and higher realities, and enables one to make right choices and decisions. Buddha taught many disciples, established monasteries, and lived to an advanced age. Buddhist teachers went to Tibet in the seventh century, and later to China and other regions of Asia. *Zen* is the Japanese pronunciation of Chinese *Ch'an*, an abbreviation of *Channa*, the Chinese rendering of Sanskrit *dhyana* (meditation). The aim of Zen practice is instantaneous enlightenment (*satori*).

> Decay is inherent in all component things. Work out your salvation with diligence. – *Words attributed to the Buddha*

Taoism (dou'ism): China

Lao-tsu taught that the Tao (dou)—"the *way*" to know the ultimate, pure Reality—is right conduct and attentive practice of the virtues of humility and compassion. Pure Reality is viewed as unmanifest: permanent and unchanging. It causes the manifestation of breath (*ch'i* or life force) which produces by movement the active principle of *yang,* and by stillness the principle of *yin* (rest). The interactions of these principles are said to produce the changing physical world. In the unmanifest realm, perfect harmony prevails; in the manifest realm, balance is disturbed.

The Taoist ideal of immortality is transcendent being, rather than endless preservation of the body. Practices that may be used by one who aspires to that state include hygienic and dietary disciplines; controlled respiration; circulation of "inner breath" (life force); transmutation of vital forces; the use of herbs and other vitalizing substances; and moral attitudes and behaviors.

The nameless is the origin of Heaven and Earth. – *Lao tzu*

First Century of the Current Era
Christianity: Palestine, Greece, Italy

The word *Christianity* is derived from *Christ*, a title given to Jesus in the New Testament to indicate that his followers considered him to be the messiah, written about in the Old Testament, who would free them from political oppression and establish an ideal social order.

Little is known about the life of Jesus or the events that occurred around him. He is now an iconic or symbolic representation of the hopes and aspirations of millions of people about which many Christian sects avidly promulgate a variety of opinions. Much of what is now taught regarding the New Testament was gradually formulated during the first three centuries of the current era by people who either believed their understanding was accurate or contrived a theology to serve their own purposes. *Theology* is the study of God and of religious views and practices or of organized, often formalized, opinions about God and God's relationship to human beings.

The first four books of the New Testament, called gospels (good tidings), were written 40 to 60 years after the public life of Jesus to inspire and encourage members of early Christian communities. The first three, which are attributed to Matthew, Mark, and Luke, are synoptic: presented from a similar viewpoint. Mark's book is believed to have been written first.

Matthew begins by describing the ancestry of Jesus from Abraham to Joseph to indicate that he is to be known as the future leader of the Jewish people, then mentions that he was born of a virgin. Luke also includes the virgin birth story. It not mentioned by Mark or John; both begin with Jesus, as an adult, being baptized.

Jesus is the Greek word for Joshua, or Yeshu. Christ, the descriptive title, is from Greek *christos* (Hebrew *Mashiah*) "to anoint." In some religious traditions, oil is put on the forehead or other parts of the body of a person who is being blessed by a priest. The Jewish followers of Jesus considered him to have been uniquely God-blessed or divinely anointed.

No reliable information about Jesus' life from the age of twelve to thirty is available, though there are unverifiable stories about his travels to India and Tibet to study with saints and sages during those "missing years." Many historians think that Jesus was born (3 BCE), during a spring month, because shepherds were then watching over their flocks (*Luke 2:8*). Shepherds guarded their sheep day and night only in spring when lambs were being born. During the winter months their sheep were kept in a corral.

The idea of observing the birth of Jesus in December was first considered in the fourth century. Mithraism, a rival pagan religion, celebrated *Natalis Solis Invicti* (Birthday of the Invincible Sun God, Mithras) during the winter equinox when the sun's movement toward the south indicated the coming of the spring growing season. The word *pagan* (Latin *pagamus*, a country-dweller) was used to refer to anyone who was not a Christian, Jew, or an adherent of a formal religion. Mithraism was so popular with the masses that in 274 Emperor Aurlian made it the official Roman religion. Church leaders, wanting to replace Mithraism with Christian influences, decided to celebrate the birth of Jesus on what is now December 25. Christmas (Christ Mass) was firmly established in 337, a little more than two decades after Christianity was proclaimed the official Roman state religion in 313.

A Christian Easter celebration was patterned after Estre, an annual pagan event named for the Saxon goddess of spring and offspring. Christians who didn't celebrate Estre with their neighbors were looked upon with disfavor. The Easter celebration was scheduled during the Estre event so that Christian gatherings could be in accord with those of members of their "pagan" community, and to perhaps attract some converts.

Various opinions have been published regarding the story of the crucifixion and resurrection of Jesus. According to New Testament accounts, Jesus was killed because his popularity with the people threatened the political influence of their Roman rulers. Some historians believe that Jesus did not die on the cross; that he was put in a tomb alive, recovered, privately met with disciples for several weeks, went to north India (or somewhere else), and lived to an advanced age. A stone tomb in Kashmir is said by some of the local people to contain the body of Jesus. That this might be true is not a comforting idea for Christians who have been told that Jesus died to atone for their sins—especially the stain of "original sin"—which they were told that every person is born with because of Eve's willfulness, and especially her dalliance with Adam in the Garden of Eden.

Early Church theologians were preoccupied with the idea of sin: human faults or errors, especially in regard to religious or moral laws and sexual misconduct. Because they presumed the

Garden of Eden allegory to be about sexual matters, and men and women are instinctually inclined to mate, they considered sexual intercourse to be impure. That is why they emphasized the presumed virginity of the mother of Jesus and the need for all people, even infants and small children, to be cleansed of the far-reaching effects of Eve's faulty behavior.

Ritual sacrificing of animals to appease the gods was a common practice in that era. Saying that the death of Jesus could atone for the sins of Christians was a convenient way to encourage them to embrace the new religion. Many Christians who now profess to believe this would be offended, if not repulsed, if asked to participate in a ceremonial "shedding of blood" of an animal to obtain forgiveness for their misdeeds.

The doctrines of original sin and of the trinity are not to be found in the New Testament. Jesus (Joshua, son of Joseph), was a Palestinian rabbi who openly interacted with members of Jewish communities and encouraged them to adhere to their traditional, cultural customs and religious observances. The much later, widely circulated opinions of the self-proclaimed apostle, Paul, who did not personally know Jesus, were strongly influential in shaping the views which are now widely promulgated in the name of Christianity.

The New Testament has been translated into many languages with a variety of interpretations of meanings of words, stories, and sayings attributed to individuals. Unless a person can read the original versions—and has an understanding of the cultural conditions, and of how people lived and thought two thousand years ago—it is unlikely that a comprehensive grasp of what is read will be possible. In that era, the books of Matthew, Mark, Luke, and John, and letters of the apostles (traveling missionaries), were often copied by scribes who sometimes made mistakes, left out words or sentences, supplemented the text with their own thoughts or versions of a story, or even embellished the text with a story that was not in the original version.

An example of embellishment is the story in John's book (8th chapter) about a woman accused of adultery. Some men brought her to Jesus to hear what he would say when they asked him what should be done with her. Killing a woman by throwing rocks was the usual punishment at the time. Jesus is portrayed as writing on the ground, perhaps as a way to have time to think about the matter. The problem is easily solved when he says, "He that is without sin among you, let him first cast a stone at her." The men, now "convicted by their own conscience," silently depart. This story, which illustrates the virtue of forgiveness, is a frequent sermon-theme and has been dramatized in films and television shows, is not in the original text of John's book, nor is it mentioned elsewhere in the New Testament. It is thought to have been written by an anonymous scribe or copyist who was inclined to embellish the text or had heard the story from someone else.

While the early Church was still in its formative stages, it had to compete with other, appealing religious teachings. One was Gnosticism: the doctrine of Christian sects that valued inquiry into spiritual truth above blind faith in a religious doctrine. Gnostics considered salvation to be attainable only by those whose accurate knowledge of higher realities enabled them to transcend material circumstances.

The teachings attributed to Jesus in the New Testament are not original. The cultivation of moral virtues, forgiveness, compassionate behavior, renunciation of egotism, aspiration to be spiritually conscious, prayer, and meditative contemplation, were taught by many inspired men and women before and during the era in which Jesus lived.

> You shall know the truth, and the truth shall make you free.
> – *The Gospel of John 8:32*

Islam: Saudi Arabia

Founded 622 CE by Muhammad. *Islam* is the Arabic word for "surrender." The Koran (*Qu'ran*) is the revered scripture of devout Muslims who pray five times each day and sincerely endeavor to do God's will.

In God I put my trust. – *The Koran 9:129*

Most of the established religions have a variety of sects whose adherents privately or openly profess different creeds (beliefs or opinions) and the importance of their ritual observances and lifestyle preferences. Some have esoteric teachings which are offered only to special individuals within the body of believers and are not publicly disclosed. A few have had, and still have, mystics: individuals who fervently aspire to directly experience and know God by prayer and/or meditative contemplation.

Because religious doctrines and philosophical concepts are usually influenced by the personal experiences, opinions, and cultural and societal circumstances of persons who originated or proclaimed them, they should be carefully, intellectually, and intuitively examined until what is true is accurately discerned. While naive acceptance of what others believe, say, or do may temporarily pacify the mind and provide a degree of emotional satisfaction, it does not fully satisfy the desire to have flawless knowledge of one's essence of being and higher realities.

Within the past one hundred and fifty years, several new religious movements have been formed; some with characteristics of formal religions, and others which emphasize the ideal of nurturing spirituality rather than adherence to traditional views and practices. Some of these organized movements, that evolved in Japan, South America, and the United States, have attracted millions of followers, and through their literature and outreach endeavors have influenced many more people who are not formally identified with them. Unity School of Practical Christianity, Religious Science, Divine Science, and other more recently established movements with thriving churches and learning centers throughout America and in other countries, promulgate a teaching emphasis referred to as New Thought. Its adherents emphasize constructive thinking, holistic living, the possibility of spiritual healing, and the freedom of everyone to independently investigate ultimate realities.

During the past few decades many people, especially in the United States and Europe, have been actively involved in what is called a New Age approach to self-actualization. Many adherents of this trend are attracted to the practical and beneficial practices of holistic living, positive thinking, physical exercise, hatha yoga or other life-enhancing routines, and meditation. Others are primarily interested in unproductive involvements, such as channeling (a modern word for spiritualism), hypnosis, magical rituals, eliciting past life memories, diet fads, seminars or teachings that are vigorously promoted as ways to "quick spiritual enlightenment," or endeavors to soon bring forth an era of global enlightenment by visualization or prayer.

Among adherents of traditional religious groups as well as the more liberal thinkers, an undercurrent of expectation persists regarding the possibility that a world teacher or savior-figure may soon emerge to spiritually awaken people and bring order and harmony into the world.

To idolize or worship spiritually enlightened people, past or present, is a grievous mistake because it fosters an illusion of great difference between them and us. What is needed, and is now occurring, is for more people to acknowledge their own spiritual essence and attend to effective practices which can allow their innate qualities and capacities to be actualized.

Recommended Reading and Sources

While having a broad range of valid knowledge may not directly contribute to our spiritual growth, it can enable us to more fully understand the processes of life, make wiser choices, live gracefully, and more effectively relate to others and the world in which we live.

A list of Roy Eugene Davis' books is on page 2.

Autobiography of a Yogi. Paramahansa Yogananda. Self-Realization Fellowship, Los Angeles.

Sacred Origins of Profound Things. Charles Panati. Arkana, The Penquin Publishing Group, New York.

The Great Transformation: The Beginning of Our Religious Traditions. Karen Armstrong. A Borzoi Book by Alfred A. Knopf, New York.

Misquoting Jesus: The Story Behind Who Changed the Bible and Why. Bart D. Ehrman. Harper San Francisco.

Abingdon Dictionary of Living Religions. Keith Crim, general editor. Abingdon, Nashville.

Ayurveda: The Science of Self-Healing. Vasant Lad. Lotus Press, Santa Fe, New Mexico.

Textbook of Ayurveda: Fundamental Principles. Vasant Lad. The Ayurvedic Press, Albuquerque, New Mexico.

On Food and Cooking: The Science and Lore of the Kitchen. A comprehensive explanation of foods, their sources and characteristics, and how they are transformed by cooking. Revised and updated edition, 2004. Harald McGee. Scribner, New York.

Science and Cosmology. Books or articles by or about Albert Einstein in which his theories of general and special relativity are described, and other sources of valid information about the universe and the processes of Nature.

Glossary

absolute Perfect in nature or quality, complete. Not mixed: pure. Not limited by restrictions: unconditional.

actualize To make real by actions. Goals are actualized when they are accomplished. Abilities are actualized when they are expressed.

affirm Latin *affirmare*, to strengthen. To declare to be true.

agnosticism The theory that, while not denying the existence of God, asserts that God cannot be known and that only objective phenomena are objects of real knowledge.

ashram A secluded, quiet place for study and spiritual practice that provides a supportive environment where spiritual aspirants can live without distractions.

astral realm The realm of life forces and energies.

astrology The study of the positions and aspects of planets and their possible influence on world events and in human affairs.

atheism Disbelief in or denial of the existence of God as a person.

avatar An incarnation of divine qualities and powers. A spiritually enlightened soul said to incarnate to impart divine influences into human affairs and planetary consciousness. The impersonal "universal avatar" concept is that divine qualities of individuals become more pronounced as their consciousness becomes illumined.

awareness The capacity to perceive. Blurred awareness is the cause of illusions (erroneous concepts or beliefs resulting from flawed perception of what is observed).

ayurveda Sanskrit *ayus*, life; *veda*, knowledge. The natural way to nurture total well-being that evolved in India thousands of years ago. Diagnostic procedures include examination of the patient's pulse, body temperature, skin, eyes, psychological characteristics, mental attitude, behaviors, and other factors. Treatment may include foods and herbs for specific purposes, attitude adjustment, behavior modification, detoxification regimens, meditation practice, and other procedures that may restore balance to the basic mind-body constitution.

The basic mind-body constitution is said to be regulated by three governing principles (*vata*, space-air influence; *pitta*, fire influence; *kapha*, water-earth influence). Foods are chosen according to their tastes (sweet, sour, salty, pungent, bitter, and astringent). Food transformation is said to progress through eight stages: plasma, blood, muscle, fat, bone, bone marrow, reproductive essences, and a fine energy-essence (*ojas*) that strengthens the immune system.

In the *Charaka Samhita*, an early ayurvedic text, medicinal uses of more than five hundred herbs are described. Knowledge of ayurvedic practices spread from India to Tibet, China, and Mediterranean countries, and recently to Europe and the Americas. During British rule in India, ayurvedic practices declined in urban areas but continued to be the wellness treatment of choice among rural populations. Several ayurvedic colleges have been established in India in recent years and clinics in many countries now provide ayurvedic services.

Siddha medicine, a similar wellness system, evolved in south India. Its texts are believed to have been written by enlightened saints (*siddhas*), among whom Agastya is especially revered. Practitioners of this system may also prescribe the ashes of gems and purified metals for healing and rejuvenation.

being The quality or state of existence. The basic, essential nature. Philosophical definition: absolute existence in its perfect, unqualified state.

Bhagavad Gita Holy or divine song: *bhaj*, to revere or love, *gai*, song. It is an allegory, a story in which characters, objects, and events symbolically illustrate an ideal or a moral or religious principle.

Krishna, a central character, represents enlightened consciousness that reveals "the eternal way of righteousness" to the student, Arjuna, with emphasis on the importance of acquiring knowledge of higher realities, selfless service, devotion, and meditation.

bliss The pure joy of awareness of being, rather than a happy mental state or an emotion.

buddhi Verb-root *budh*, to know. A spiritually enlightened person is said to be a buddha: one who knows the truth about life. Because souls are units of one Reality, everyone has a "buddha nature" at the core of their being.

capacity The ability to receive, hold, or absorb.

categories of cosmic manifestation One Reality eternally exists. Its absolute aspect is changeless; its expressive aspects are subject to being modified and changed in accord with the states or combined influences of three, primary attributes (*gunas*) which can influence cosmic forces. When the three gunas are in a state of equilibrium, manifestation of cosmic forces does not occur. When tamas guna (inertia) is influential, a vibration (Om) of the power of supreme Consciousness is emanated in which time, space, and fine cosmic forces are produced. From this unified field of primordial nature, electric and magnetic forces are projected as five subtle element-influences: space with cosmic forces; air (gaseous elements); fire; water; and earth, which interact to produce physical matter. The five fine element-influences are said to be the true essences of the physical universe. Physical manifestation of the elements is said to occur when half of a subtle element-influence combines with one eighth of each of the other four element-influences.

causal realm The electric, and magnetic forces emanated from the field of primordial nature that produce the astral and physical realms.

chakra Sanskrit "wheel." Seven major astral centers are in the spine and brain, each with unique attributes. *See Chapter Three.*

channeling A modern word for mediumship: the belief that souls which have departed from this world can be contacted by telepathic or other means for the purpose of communication. Some people try to contact souls in astral realms to prove their existence or hope to acquire higher knowledge. People who claim to do this are either self-deceived or dishonest. They should concentrate on actualizing their own divine qualities.

chanting The intoning or singing of a simple, melodic lyric. Studies indicate that chanting can reduce stress, calm the mind, and result in harmonious interactions between the hemispheres of the brain.

compassion Empathetic concern for suffering or misfortune of others, together with an inclination to give aid or support.

concentration An undisturbed flow of attention.

conscience The ability to recognize the difference between right and wrong regarding one's conduct, with knowledge that one should act accordingly. Compliant conformance to a sense of proper conduct.

consciousness The capacity to be self-aware, observe, and perceive. The totality of one's memories, thoughts, beliefs, and sensitivities to respond or react to objective or subjective conditions.

contemplate Latin *con*, intensive; *templum*, a space for observing something. To examine or consider to be possible. To alertly "look at" with hopeful expectation of discovery.

cosmic consciousness Awareness and understanding of the unified wholeness of life.

cosmic mind The one, universal mind of which all minds are units or parts. Mental states, subliminal tendencies and urges, thoughts, desires, and intentions interact with cosmic mind which is inclined to responsively express corresponding events and circumstances.

decisive Characterized by determined or resolute choice.

deism The belief that God created the universe, but is apart from it, has no influence on phenomena, and provides no revelation.

delusion An erroneous idea, concept, or belief.

desire To wish for or want. Desires enable us to achieve goals and accomplish purposes. Life-enhancing desires that contribute to well-being are acceptable. Nonuseful desires or obsessive cravings that interfere with rational thinking, cause emotional unrest, or are allowed to impel unwise or erratic behaviors, should be avoided or replaced with wholesome, life-enhancing desires.

destiny An inevitable, predetermined occurrence. It is the destiny of all souls to be spiritually enlightened and liberated.

devotion Strong attraction. Attachment, loyalty.

dharma That which upholds and supports the processes of life and empowers evolution. *Dharmic living* is in harmony with the cosmic order. To adhere to one's path in life in accord with the orderly processes of nature is to fulfill one's dharma: aims and purposes that are constructive and meaningful.

disciple Latin *discipulus* < *discere*, to learn. An adherent of a philosophical system or spiritual tradition.

ego An illusional (mistaken) sense of self.

egotism An inflated or exaggerated sense of self-importance dramatized as a strong sense of individualism and arrogant willfulness.

elicit To bring forth. Physical relaxation, mental calmness, spiritual qualities, and superconscious states may be elicited by decisive intention and by attentive meditation practice.

emotion A subjective feeling-response to something observed or experienced. Thoughts, memories, smells, tastes, the behaviors or words of others, or observation of objective events or circumstances may elicit feelings of attraction, aversion, fear, insecurity, sadness, loneliness, desire, confidence, happiness, security, well-being, compassion, or other emotional responses. Emotional stability and maturity provide a firm foundation for spiritual growth.

enlightenment To be provided with spiritual wisdom or insight.

era A duration of time. *See yuga.*

essence The fundamental properties that identify or characterize something. Its inherent, unchanging nature.

evil Common usage: morally wrong, harmful, or causing misfortune. The basic sense of the word is thought to have been "exceeding proper bounds" or "overreaching." It did not signify merely the absence of good. There are no cosmic evil forces or influences.

evolution A process, usually gradual, in which something changes to a different or more complex form. The theory that groups of organisms, as species, may change over time so that descendants differ structurally and physiologically from their ancestors.

facilitate To make easier. Holistic living, rational thinking, having accurate knowledge of higher realities, and superconscious meditation practice facilitate psychological transformation and spiritual growth.

faith Confident belief in the truth, value, or trustworthiness of something. Belief not based on proof or material evidence. Religious or spiritual conviction.

field A place in which events occur. A region of space indicated by physical properties such as gravitational or electromagnetic forces. Our awareness is a field. Cosmic mind is a field. The Oversoul and primordial nature are fields.

God The absolute Reality is existence-being. The expressive aspect (Cosmic Soul) has three constituent attributes (gunas) which pervade its vibrating power (Om) and the universe.

 The word *god* (German "the highest good") is derived from an Indo-European language in which an ancestor form meant "the invoked one." The only surviving non-Germanic relative is Sanskrit *hu* ("invoke the Gods"), a form of which is in the Rig-Veda (Hymn of Knowledge) is *puru-hutas* ("much invoked"). *Brahma* indicates the expanding, creation-producing aspect of supreme Consciousness. *Brahman* indicates absolute supreme Consciousness.

 Muslims devoted to the ideal of submission to God use *Allah* (al-Lah), The Great Adored. Christians use the words *God, Heavenly Father*, and *Lord*. The names used to refer to God often reflect what people imagine to be the highest attribute of deity. Zoroastrians in ancient Persia (Iran) used *Ahura Mazda*, The Wise Creator. In Hinduism, some aspects of deity are characterized according to their presumed influences or roles. *Divine Mother*, a nurturing influence. *Ishwara*, ruler or regulator of the cosmic order. *Shiva*, transformative and regenerative. *Vishnu*, preserver of cosmic order. *Saraswati*, goddess of speech and learning; *Lakshmi*, goddess of prosperity and good fortune. *Goddesses* are depicted as creative energies of the gods (unique influences of cosmic forces).

Godhead The Cosmic Soul of supreme Consciousness from which the vibrating power that produces and sustains universes is emanated.

grace Freely provided benefits, good fortune, or support.

gunas The three constituent attributes of the Cosmic Soul which, pervading the primordial field of nature and the universe, regulate cosmic forces. Their influences are: 1) purifying and illuminating (sattwic); 2) transformative (rajasic); 3) inertial (tamasic).

guru That which removes darkness or ignorance. Teacher. One who provides higher knowledge and may transmit transformative spiritual energies to the receptive disciple.

hallucination A false or distorted perception of something. Mind- or brain-produced phenomena without any real basis.

heal To make whole. To restore to complete health, well-being, or spiritual wholeness.

heart Physiology: the muscular organ in the thoracic cavity that pumps blood. Metaphysical: the essence of a person's being and sensibilities; one's true Self. When seers advise a person to "seek the truth in your heart" they mean that the essence of their being is to be meditatively contemplated and realized (directly experienced and known).

heaven Originally a cosmological term used to refer to a region of the universe, and later used to indicate religious idealism. In ancient Middle Eastern thought, heaven was imagined as a region of the cosmos beyond which was a transcendent realm. In ancient Greek mythology, Zeus was depicted as dwelling on Mount Olympus.

Writers of the books of The Old Testament thought of heaven as God's abode from which sovereign rule was exercised and to which the faithful righteous would be eventually welcomed. The New Testament indicates a modified version of heaven as a creation of God in which God resides, as well as a final condition of blessedness to be experienced by the spiritually prepared. Christians (and other adherents of religious traditions) teach various concepts of heaven.

Hinduism A word coined by foreigners who invaded India. *See the Addendum: The Evolution of Religious Beliefs and Practices.*

holistic Emphasis on the importance of the wholeness of something and the interdependence of its parts and processes.

holy Considered to be of divine origin or character.

humility Absence of egotism.

illusion Latin *illusio*, an imitation. A mistaken perception of subjective or objective realities.

imagination A mental picture or concept of a thing, event, situation, or circumstance. Creative imagining is intentional or controlled. Fantasy is uncontrolled imagining.

infinite Without boundaries or limits.

initiation Latin *initium*, beginning < *inire*, to go in. A new beginning. A rite of passage into a body of knowledge and the company of adherents of that knowledge.

innate Inborn: possessed from the beginning as an essential characteristic; inherent.

inspire Latin *inspirare*: *in-*, into, and *spirare*, to breath. To be inspired is to be affected, or aroused by divine influence.

intellect The faculty of discrimination or discernment.

intensive Concentrated, focused.

intuition Direct perception without the aid of the senses.

karma An influence that causes or may cause an effect. Accumulated subconscious conditionings, tendencies, habits, mental attitudes, behaviors, inclinations, expectations, and desires are included in one's personal karmic condition. Life-enhancing influences may be allowed to be helpful. Harmful influences can be resisted, weakened, and neutralized by implementing constructive thinking, feelings, and behaviors. Discordant personal relationships can be harmonized or renounced. Harmful environmental influences should be avoided when possible, or transcended.

kriya Sanskrit "action" or process that can produce a desired effect.

kriya yoga Disciplined thinking and behaviors, profound study of higher realities and discovery of one's essence of being, and seeing through or rising above the false sense of one's essence of being. Kriya yoga practices are described in Patanjali's yoga-sutras.

kundalini Soul force, which is mostly dormant in people who are not yet spiritually awake. In spiritually awake individuals, its energies are enlivening and transformative. It can be aroused by aspiration to spiritual growth, devotion, meditation, being in places where spiritual influences prevail, and mental and spiritual attunement with someone who is spiritually awake.

laws of cause and effect Invariable relationships that exist between or among phenomena when specific conditions prevail. The laws of cause and effect influence cosmic processes and produce events that create circumstances.

life The properties or qualities expressed in growth, metabolism, response to stimuli, and reproduction. The physical, mental, and spiritual experiences that make up one's sense of existence.

light Electromagnetic radiation that travels 186,282 miles a second in a vacuum; approximately 5.878 trillion miles (9.46 trillion kilometers) in one year. The sun's radiation travels 93 million miles to Earth in approximately eight minutes. The spectrum of red, orange, yellow, green, blue, indigo and violet is visible to humans. Red is produced by a low frequency, long wave; violet by a high frequency, short wave. TV and radio wavelengths are below red. Ultraviolet, X-rays, and gamma rays are beyond violet. All electromagnetic radiations are called light. When an electron in an atom is impacted by radiation or collides with another atom, it receives energy which is either absorbed or emitted as a photon (particle) of a specific wavelength. A wavelength is the distance in a periodic wave between two points of corresponding phases in consecutive cycles.

love Affection or fondness for someone or a living thing.

mantra Sanskrit *manas*, mind, and *tra*, to protect. A sound, word, or word-phrase used to focus attention, especially when meditating.

master Latin *magister*. One who is acknowledged as being proficient in a branch of learning or has unique skills or abilities. A master of yoga has complete control over mental and emotional states, states of consciousness, sensory impulses, and vital forces.

material A substance of which something is made.

matter Confined energy that occupies space.

maya That which measures, defines, limits, and can produce forms of matter; the characteristics of the primordial field of nature.

meditation An undisturbed flow of attention to an object or ideal one aspires to identify with or realize. Detachment of attention and awareness from external conditions, senses, emotions, and mental states that enables one to realize (directly experience and know) their pure-conscious essence of being and the reality of God.

metaphysics Latin *metaphysica* < Greek *tà metà tà physiká*, "the things after the physics." The title given to Aristotle's treatise on first principles written after his treatise on physics. The branch of philosophy that investigates first principles of ultimate reality, including the nature of being and cosmology.

mind Sanskrit *manas*, to think.

mind-body constitution Formed by inherited characteristics, prenatal and postnatal environmental influences, and one's karmic condition when born. The three governing principles of biological and psychological processes are *vata* (air or flowing movements); *pitta* (fire that influences chemical, biological, and psychological transformation); *kapha* (moisture and denser substances that lubricate and nourish). Indications of balanced vata influences are efficient elimination of waste products, a strong immune system, orderly functioning of the body's systems, emotional stability, and sound sleep. Indications of balanced pita influences are strong powers of digestion, vitality, intellectual acuity, decisiveness, and self-confidence. Some indications of balanced kapha influences are physical strength, serenity, firm resolve to do something, rational thinking, patience, strong endurance, and adaptability. When the mind-body constitution is balanced, physical and psychological health can prevail. When it is not balanced, physical or psychological distress may be experienced. Balance may be restored and maintained by attitude adjustment, behavior modification, food choices, therapeutic regimens, and cultivation of spiritual awareness. *See ayurveda.*

miracle An event that seems impossible to explain by natural laws because the natural laws that caused it are not generally known.

modify To change the character of something or to restrict or limit. Awareness is modified by accumulated information, false beliefs, misperceptions (illusions), sleep, memories, and fantasies.

mysticism Belief in the existence of realities beyond ordinary powers of perception which are accessible by subjective experience, as by intuition. Spiritual disciplines that are practiced to unify attention and awareness with one's true nature and God or ultimate Reality, usually by means of contemplative meditation. The experience of such realization.

nadi A channel or conduit through which prana (life force) flows. *Ida nadi*, the left channel in the spine, is a lunar (cooling) influence. *Pingala*, the right channel, is a solar (heating) influence. Life force moves through *sushumna nadi*, the central channel, when attention is internalized or when certain methods (such as kriya pranayama) are used. In sushumna nadi are two astral channels and a fine channel of consciousness-matter.

New Thought A modern movement whose adherents emphasize constructive thinking, holistic living, and independent investigation of higher realities.

ojas Refined energy that strengthens the body's immune system; the final product of food transformation. It is increased by mental calmness, wholesome living, spiritual practices, and transmutation of vital forces.

Om The vibration of the power of Consciousness.

omnipotence Unlimited power.

omnipresence Present everywhere.

omniscience All knowing.

ordinary Common, usual. Not exceptional.

paramahansa *Para*, beyond or transcendent; *hansa*, swan. One who is considered to be a spiritual master, a free soul no longer limited by karma or illusions, whose wisdom-impelled actions are always appropriate. As a swan has an earthly abode and can soar free in the sky, a paramahansa can be in the world without being confined by its conditions. Mythology: a swan is said to be able to extract milk from a mixture of milk and water. A paramahansa is said to relate only to divine essences while living in the material realm without restrictions.

patience Calm endurance of transitory events and circumstances by being peacefully soul-centered.

philosophy Latin *philosophia* < Greek *philosophos*. The love and seeking of wisdom by diligent, disciplined inquiry.

prana Life force. A soul's life force blends with the body at the medulla oblongata at the base of the brain. When prana flows freely, health prevails. When flows are imbalanced, weak, or disturbed, psychological or physical discomfort or distress may occur. Pranayama practice balances prana-flows in the body. Alternate nostril breathing, described in chapter three of the text, may be used to balance the flows of prana in the left and right channels in the spinal pathway.

pranayama Regulation of breathing rhythms to harmonize flows of life force in the body and calm the mind as preparation for meditation.

prayer Latin *precaria*, to obtain by entreaty or request. The act of making such a request. Reverent petitioning of God for something that is desired or needed. *See chapter six.*

primordial nature The first field of cosmic manifestation in which Om and Om's self-expressed aspects—space, time, and fine cosmic forces—are unified.

prosperous Having success; thriving. Continuous emergence of fortunate events and ideal circumstances spontaneously occur when the spiritual, mental, emotional, physical, and environmental components of one's life are harmoniously integrated.

psyche Latin from Greek, soul. In most Western cultures the psyche is usually viewed as the mind being the center of thought, feeling, and behavior, and adjusting and relating the body to its social and physical environment.

psychic Of or relating to the soul or to extraordinary powers of perception.

realization Experience along with accurate knowledge of something.

redemptive The capacity to restore, rescue, free, or liberate.

reincarnation The idea or belief that souls repeatedly incarnate to have experiences in the physical realm. It is not spiritually beneficial to be preoccupied with thoughts about possible past incarnations that one may presume to have had. Attention and endeavors should instead be focused on authentic spiritual growth that will result in liberation of consciousness.

renunciation Discarding mental and emotional attachments to things, places, circumstances, emotional states, memories, actions, and the results of actions. Most easily done by concentrating on purposes that have real value.

sage A wise person.

saint A person whose divine qualities are actualized.

salvation Liberation of consciousness. Freedom from pain, discomfort, or spiritual ignorance—which may be temporary or permanent as determined by one's degree of spiritual awareness. Limited salvation is a condition in which Self-realization is not yet flawless or permanent. Subliminal inclinations, erroneous beliefs, or illusions may still be influential. When all limitations are removed or transcended and awareness is clear, liberation is permanent.

samadhi From Sanskrit *sam*, "the bringing together completely" of attention and awareness with an object of meditative contemplation. During preliminary or lower samadhi, attention and awareness are supported by perceptions of what is seen or felt. Pure samadhi is not supported by an object.

Sanskrit The refined or "polished" language from which many Indo-European languages were derived. Prominent in India during the Vedic era, it is now being more widely studied and used. The Sanskrit alphabet is considered to be a mantra, with sound-phrases of spiritual significance and powers which have the seed-frequencies of creation. A sound (*shabda*) is said have a power (*shakti*) which conveys a meaning which is inseparably related to the sound. The sound-element behind audible sounds is the fundamental sound (*sphota*). Contemplation of a subtle sound-element or seed (*bija*) reveals its true essence. Sanskrit mantras are believed to be uniquely effective in facilitating spiritual awakening. The potency of mantras is derived from Om, the primordial sound continuously emanating from the Godhead and expressive in the universe.

satan An ancient Hebrew word for an obstruction or something which causes difficulties. Ancient religious people attempted to define an array of unseen presences imagined as having power to affect human beings and everyday events: gods, demigods, angels, demons, and ghosts. Some imagined influences were viewed as benevolent, others, as harmful. When the Old Testament was translated into Greek in the third century BCE, *satan* was translated as *diabolus* (French *diable*; German *teuful*; English *devil*). The first known endeavor to concentrate all evil in a single, personal form occurred before the sixth century BCE, in Persia, given the name *Ahiriman* and described as the Principle of Darkness engaged in ceaseless conflict with the Principle of Light for control of the world. This version of a personified evil influence was adapted from Persian concepts by Jewish religious thinkers and by early Christians. The fact that satanic influences do not exist has not yet persuaded millions of people to abandon this erroneous idea.

science Disciplined observation, precise identification, and experimental investigation of mundane phenomena or other realities.

seer One who accurately discerns the truth of what is observed.

Self An individualized unit of pure consciousness; the real essence of one's being. When it is identified with mental modifications and a mistaken sense of self, it is referred to as a soul. Units are individualized by the blending of the radiance of supreme Consciousness with characteristics of primordial nature. Self-realization is actualized when the difference between one's pure essence of being and modified states of awareness is directly experienced.

shakti The expressive energy of kundalini.

shaktipat Arousal of kundalini energies, which may spontaneously occur. It may also occur because of a person's spiritual practice, their mental or spiritual attunement, or physical contact with someone whose kundalini energies are already awakened.

siddha A spiritually accomplished person. One whose innate qualities and capacities are fully actualized.

siddhis Exceptional powers of perception and extraordinary abilities one may have when partially or more fully spiritually awake. They can be used to live more effectively and to complete one's spiritual awakening to liberation of consciousness.

soul A unit of pure consciousness with blurred awareness that is not yet aware of its pure-conscious essence.

space Infinite extension of three-dimensional reality in which events occur.

spiritual Of or related to God and souls.

spiritual eye The sixth chakra, in the forehead. Light may be perceived here when a meditator's mind is calm. *See chapter three.*

stage A level, degree, or period of time in the course of an ongoing process or procedure.

subjective Produced by or existing in the mind.

subliminal Below the threshold of conscious awareness. Subliminal influences activate thoughts and emotions. When they cease to be influential, the mind is calm and awareness is clear.

superconscious Latin *super*, above, over. Of superior quality. A clear state of consciousness superior to ordinary awake states, dream states, and sleep.

swami A member of the ancient monastic order reorganized by Adi (the first) Shankara in the seventh century. A swami renounces mundane attachments, selflessly works for the welfare of others, and (usually) engages in spiritual practices.

technique A systematic procedure. A meditation technique may be used to elicit relaxation, calm the mind, and focus attention.

time An interval between events. Part of a continuum which includes space and cosmic forces, no part of which can be distinguished from the others except by arbitrary division for the purpose of analysis or theoretical speculation.

Our sense of time is related to events: pendulums swing; quartz crystals vibrate; atoms, forms of light, electric and magnetic fields, and planets move. What is time like where objective realities do not exist? In an absolute void, only that Something which makes relative happenings possible exists.

The interval of time we call a year marks one movement of Earth around the sun. A day is one spin of Earth on its axis. A month was formerly related to the duration of the orbit of the moon. Astronomical measures of time are not always absolute. When the moon was farther away from the earth, many thousands of years ago, its orbit was longer. Days and years are variable. A seven-day week is an arbitrary designation. Other cultures have had five, eight, and ten day weeks. Until the fourteenth century, days had irregular intervals of morning, noon, evening, and night. Summer daylight hours are longer than winter daylight hours. Hours, minutes, and time zones were standardized when it became necessary to coordinate train and travel schedules.

At the Equator, the Earth's rate of spin is 1,000 miles an hour. Its speed around the sun is almost 20 miles a second (72,000 miles an hour). Our solar system in relationship to the center of our galaxy is moving at 120 miles a second (432,000 miles an hour). Our galaxy is moving toward the galaxy Andromeda at 50 miles a second (180,000 miles an hour).

Time need not be thought of as an obstacle to spiritual growth. While psychological transformations, refinements of the nervous system, and other changes that may be necessary to accommodate higher states of consciousness occur in time, it is possible to transcend concepts of time.

transcendent Beyond the limits of ordinary human ability to access or comprehend. It can be intuitively perceived or directly experienced.

Transcendental field Absolute Consciousness, pure existence-being without characteristics.

transcendentalism The belief that knowledge of higher realities may be intuitively perceived or directly experienced rather than acquired only by examination of objective circumstances.

truth Conformity to fact or actuality.

upanishad Sanskrit, "to sit down" near the teacher. Two hundred upanishads exist, of which 108 are the most widely known. Lesser known are the *yoga-upanishads*, which describe a variety of practices. Some early upanishads were composed as far back as 900 BCE. The usual form of presentation of information is conversational, depicting a wise teacher responding to questions asked by a truth seeker.

veda Knowledge, especially as a revelation or insight rather than acquired by inference or other modes of analysis.

Vedas The oldest known body of religious scriptures which emerged in India more than three thousand years ago. The common theme is that one Reality exists, and can be known.

wisdom Understanding of what is true, right, and enduring.

yantra A symbolic, geometrical drawing that indicates the actions and influences of cosmic forces. *Sri* (auspicious) *Yantra* is used for meditative contemplation. With circles triangles, and lotus petals in a square that contains cosmic forces, it portrays the interactions of the forces and creative powers of supreme Consciousness.

yoga Sanskrit *yug*, to yoke or join together. *Samadhi* or oneness in Patanjali's yoga-sutras. Practices that enable a person to be Self- and God-realized.

When the philosophical concepts and practices of yoga evolved is not known. Patanjali's' yoga-sutras, written circa 200 CE, indicate that they are those of an "ancient tradition."

Hatha Yoga practice includes postures (*asanas*) to improve physical strength and flexibility and pranayamas and other procedures to enliven and regulate vital forces. It should progress to meditation practice that culminates in Self- and God-realization.

Bhakti yoga is the way of devotion.

Karma yoga is the way selfless work or action.

Jnana (*gyana*) yoga is the way of intellectual discernment of the difference between what is true and what is not true.

Raja yoga is the way of meditative contemplation and cultivation of superconsciousness.

Kriya yoga, laya yoga (meditating in Om), kundalini yoga, and other designated systems often include the effective practices of all of the yoga systems, with emphasis on specific or unique practices.

yuga An era or designated duration of time. Many centuries ago, Vedic astronomer-seers taught a theory of time-cycles to explain the effects of cosmic forces on human beings and the emergence and decline of civilizations. Each descending and ascending cycle is half of a complete 24,000 year cycle. The theory of cosmic cycles published by Sri Yukteswar in 1895 (*see chapter two*) is based on the idea that forces radiating from the center of our galaxy influence the electromagnetic fields of the solar system and the mental and intellectual faculties of our planet's human inhabitants. When our solar system is most distant from the center of our galaxy, mental, intellectual, and intuitive powers of most people are weak, soul awareness is dim, and inability to comprehend the facts of life is common. When our solar system is nearest to the galactic center, mental, intellectual, and intuitive powers of more people become highly developed and their spiritual capacities are unveiled.

Because of a mistake in calculating the progression of cycles (circa 700 BCE), many people now mistakenly believe the current era to be a dark age of confusion.

The consciousness and intellectual capacities of dedicated spiritual aspirants are not unduly influenced by external events.

Calendar of Descending and Ascending Eras

11,500 BCE: Start of 4,800-year descending satya yuga. Thought to be the period of the beginning of civilizations.

6700 BCE: Start of 3,600-year descending treta yuga.

3100 BCE: Start of 2,400-year descending dwapara yuga. Migration of people from lower Russia to European countries and India. Eventual establishment of religious beliefs and practices in the Middle East and India.

700 BCE: Start of 1,200-year descending era of confusion. Emergence and formal establishment of Shintoism, Confucianism, Buddhism, Taoism, Christianity, and Islam.

500 CE: Start of 1,200 year ascending era of confusion.

1700 CE: Start of 2,400-year ascending dwapara yuga. Increase of human intellectual capacities and discoveries and practical uses of electricity and magnetism.

2001 CE: Start of the current millennium.

4100 CE: Start of ascending treta yuga. Further increase of human intellectual capacities and ability to discern the Source of cosmic forces.

7700 CE: Start of ascending satya yuga. Increase of human abilities to use powers of intuition and to have direct perceptions of higher realities. An era of planetary spiritual enlightenment.

The Author

Roy Eugene Davis has taught these philosophical principles and spiritual growth processes for more than five decades in North and South America, Europe, Japan, Africa, and India. Some of his books have been published in ten languages. He was ordained by Paramahansa Yogananda in 1951.

Center For Spiritual Awareness

Our international headquarters is located in the northeast Georgia mountains, 90 miles north of Atlanta. Quiet meditation retreats are offered from early spring until late autumn. CSA Press is the publishing department.

A free literature packet with a sample issue of *Truth Journal* magazine, listings of Mr. Davis' books, DVDs, and CDs, and meditation retreat schedules may be requested from:

Center For Spiritual Awareness
Post Office Box 7
Lakemont, Georgia 30552-0001

Telephone 706-782-4723 weekdays 8 a.m. – 3 p.m.
Fax 706-782-4560
e-mail csainc@csa-davis.org
Internet Web Site www.csa-davis.org